Moral
Decision
Making

Patrick Hannon

VERITAS

INTO THE CLASSROOM

RELIGIOUS EDUCATION IN THE LEAVING CERTIFICATE

Moral Decision Making

Patrick Hannon

Series Editors
Eoin G. Cassidy and Patrick M. Devitt

VERITAS

First published 2005 by
Veritas Publications
7/8 Lower Abbey Street
Dublin 1
Ireland
Email publications@veritas.ie
Website www.veritas.ie

ISBN 1 85390 781 2

10 9 8 7 6 5 4 3 2 1

Some of the material in this book is adapted from Patrick Hannon,
Church, State, Morality and Law, (Dublin: Gill & Macmillan, 1992) and
the agreement of the publishers is acknowledged with thanks.

'That Place' by R.S. Thomas from *Later Poems*
(London: Macmillan, 1983).

A catalogue record for this book is available from the British Library

Cover design by Bill Bolger
Printed in the Republic of Ireland by Betaprint Ltd, Dublin

*Veritas books are printed on paper made from the wood pulp of managed
forests. For every tree felled, at least one tree is planted, thereby renewing
natural resources.*

Contents

	Series Introduction	7
	Preface	17
	Introduction	19
1	What Being Moral Means	31
2	Why Be Moral?	40
3	Making Moral Decisions	46
4	Moral Dilemmas	58
5	Becoming Moral	70
6	Morality and Religion	80
7	Sources of Christian Moral Teaching	89
8	Gospel and Law	100
9	Christian Faith and Morality	111
10	Morality and Spirituality	120
11	Morality and Law	131
12	Pluralism and the Common Good	142
	Select Bibliography	151

Series Introduction

September 2003 saw the introduction of the Leaving Certificate Religious Education Syllabus by the Department of Education and Science. For those concerned to promote a religious sensibility in young Irish adults it is hard to exaggerate the importance of this event. It both represents a formal recognition by society of the value of religious education in the academic lives of second-level students, and it also reflects the importance which Irish society attaches to promoting the personal growth of students, including their spiritual and moral development. Religious education offers young people the opportunity to understand and interpret their experience in the light of a religious world-view. Furthermore, in and through an engagement with the RE Syllabus at Leaving Certificate level, students will learn a language that will enable them both to articulate their own faith experience and to dialogue with those of different faiths or non-theistic stances.

The Department of Education Syllabus is to be welcomed in that it gives recognition to the role that religious education plays in the human development of the young person. It is not an exaggeration to say that religious education is the capstone of the school's educational response to the young person's search for meaning and values. In this context, it encourages students to reflect upon their awareness of themselves as unique individuals with roots in a community network of family, friends and parish. Furthermore, it allows students to acknowledge and reflect upon their relationship to a God who cares for them and for the world in which we live. Finally, it gives students access to the universal nature of the quest for truth, beauty and goodness. Most of these themes are addressed sympathetically in the section entitled *The Search for Meaning and Values.* In particular, this section is to be welcomed because it offers the possibility for students to grapple with theistic and non-theistic world-views in a context that is hospitable to religious belief.

A critical dimension of the young person's educational journey is the growth in understanding of their own culture and the manner in which culture shapes their outlook on the world. The Religious Education Syllabus not only addresses the manner in which religion (and in particular Christianity) has shaped Irish culture over many centuries, but it also provides an extremely valuable platform from which to critique aspects of the relationship between faith and culture in the contemporary world. The section entitled *Religion: The Irish Experience* addresses the former concern by showing pupils the manner in which the Christian religion has contributed to the belief patterns and values of Irish society. It also alerts them to the depths of religious belief that predate by many centuries, even millennia, the arrival of Christianity in Ireland; and it also connects them to the cultural richness that links Ireland to the European continent. In this context, the devotional revolution that took place in Ireland (including the extraordinary growth in religious orders from 1850-1930) is a topic that could be expanded. The missionary outreach of the Catholic Church in Ireland in the last hundred years is worthy of special mention. Finally, students studying this section should be encouraged to acknowledge the ambiguities that have attended the presence of religion in Ireland over the centuries; to see on the one hand the image of an island of saints and scholars, and on the other hand to note how 'lilies that fester smell far worse than weeds'.

In examining the manner in which faith and culture interact, the sections entitled *Religion and Science* and *Religion and Gender* make a valuable contribution to the Syllabus. These sections address topical issues that were controversial in the past and continue to be problematical even today. In treating of these two topics it is obviously important to avoid stereotypes – the acceptance of unexamined assumptions that mask or over-simplify the truth to such an extent as to do a disservice to the seriousness of the issues involved. Likewise, the section on *World Religions* should be taught in a manner that is sensitive to the dangers of cultural and religious stereotypes. This section not only gives students a valuable introduction to the main religions in the world, but it also provides a cultural context for an awareness of the fact that the phenomenon of religion and the experience of religious belief is something that shapes people's understanding of themselves and their lifestyles across all cultural boundaries. Furthermore, it should never be forgotten that if, as Christians believe, God's Spirit is present in and through these religions, there is a need to study these religions precisely in order to discover aspects of God's presence in the world that has the capability to continually surprise.

In the Irish cultural context, Catholicism shapes the religious sensibilities and practices of the majority of young people. The Syllabus offers a generous acknowledgement of the importance of Christianity in the Irish context by providing two sections that focus on core aspects of the Christian faith. These are: *Christianity: origins and contemporary expressions* and *The Bible: Literature and Sacred text*. In this context, the Syllabus section on the Bible is to be welcomed. However, greater attention could be given to the role and significance of the Prophets in the Old Testament and to Paul in the New Testament. Furthermore, in studying the Bible it should never be forgotten that the primary reality is not the 'book' but rather the person of Christ and the community tradition grappling with this reality that is revealed in and through the Bible.

What is often in danger of being forgotten in an academic context is the importance of the fostering of attitudes and practices that promote personal growth. Religious education cannot be focused only on knowledge and understanding, because religion is primarily a way of celebrating life and, in particular, the spiritual dimension of life in and through the practices of worship, ritual and prayer. The Syllabus's recognition of this critical dimension of religious education through the section entitled *Worship, Ritual and Prayer* is to be welcomed. In addressing this section of the Syllabus it would be important to alert students to the great variety of spiritualities, prayer forms, mysticisms, rituals and styles of music that are to be found within the Christian tradition in order that students may have the possibility of exploring the richness of the spiritual dimension of their own tradition.

A key remit of the educational process is the fostering of moral maturity through a syllabus that allows students to engage in moral education. Not only is religious education particularly suited to facilitating this educational imperative, but the ethical character of human life is a core feature of all religions. The importance of this dimension of religious education is recognised in the provision of two sections entitled *Moral Decision-Making* and *Issues of Justice and Peace*. There is nothing optional about the challenge to promote justice and peace. However, it is a topic that can all too easily be ideologically driven. Therefore, there is a special responsibility on those teaching this section to ensure that the instances of injustice cited, and the causes of injustice proposed, are grounded in solid research.

The challenges to Catholic religion teachers
Though religious education has been an integral part of Irish second-level schools long before the foundation of the state, it

has not until now been possible to assess this work under the State examination system. The reason for this anomaly is the Intermediate Education Act (1878) which allowed for the teaching but forbade the State examination of religious education. The removal of this legal constraint on State examination of RE has provided the impetus for the introduction of the Junior Certificate Syllabus in September 2000 and the introduction of the Leaving Certificate Syllabus in September 2003. These changes are to be welcomed but they provide a number of major challenges to Catholic religion teachers that should not be minimised.

In the *first* place, Catholic religion teachers have to attend to the danger that the new Syllabus will lead to a weakening of a commitment to catechesis in second level schools. The catechetical project of faith formation is built around six key pillars: knowledge of the faith; liturgical/sacramental education; moral formation; learning to pray; education for community life, including a fostering of the ecumenical character of Christian community, and finally, missionary initiative and inter-religious dialogue. Clearly, the RE Leaving Certificate Syllabus does give attention to many of the above themes, including the key catechetical concerns of attitude or value formation and the development of commitments. However, the emphasis in the Syllabus is undoubtedly upon the acquiring of knowledge, understanding and knowledge-based skills, all of which undoubtedly place it under the rubric of religious education rather than catechesis. The religion teacher ought to value the distinctive approaches to religion reflected in both catechesis and religious education. Both are important because both contribute in distinctive ways to the religious development of the young person. Catechesis aims at maturity of faith whereas religious education aims at knowledge and understanding of the faith.

From the point of view of the religion teacher, the teaching can have a different tone at different times. On one occasion, it might have a 'showing how' or catechetical tone, one that assumes a shared faith experience and encourages active participation. At another time it can have an educational or 'explaining' tone that invites pupils to stand back from religion to a certain extent, so that they can gain a more objective understanding of what is being taught. The Religious Education Syllabus should be taught in a manner that keeps both of these approaches in balance. In a similar vein, the presence of RE on the Leaving Certificate curriculum should not distract teachers from acknowledging that the religious development of young people happens in many contexts, which are distinct, though complementary. It can take place at home, in the parish, with friends as well as in school. Furthermore, even in the school it can take place at a whole series of levels including liturgy, prayer and projects that encourage an awareness of the need to care for those in most need.

In the *second* place, teachers have to attend to the scope and range of the aims of the Syllabus, one that seeks both to introduce students to a broad range of religious traditions and to the non-religious interpretation of life, as well as providing students with the opportunity to develop an informed and critical understanding of the Christian tradition. In this context, teachers have to balance the need to promote tolerance for and mutual understanding of those of other or no religious traditions, alongside the need to give explicit attention to the Christian faith claims that Jesus is the Son of God and that he died to save us and to unite us with God and one another. Similarly, in teaching Christianity, teachers need to give attention to the role and significance of the Church from a Catholic perspective. It should never be forgotten that the idea of the Church as 'people of God', 'body of Christ' and 'temple of the Holy Spirit' is one that is at the heart of Catholic self-understanding.

In a similar vein, the Syllabus encourages students to engage critically with a wide variety of ethical codes with a view to the development of a moral maturity. Teachers will have to balance this approach with the way in which morality is viewed within the Christian tradition under the heading of discipleship – Jesus invites people to follow *him* rather than an ethical code or vision. Furthermore, from a Christian perspective, morality is never simply or even primarily concerned with a listing of moral prohibitions, rather it situates the ethical dimension of human nature within the context of a belief in a forgiving God. Finally, it should not be forgotten that it does not make sense to teach morality in too abstract a manner. Morality is something preeminently practical and at all times needs to be brought down to the level of real people – those who struggle with the demands of conscience in their lives. From a Catholic perspective, one has in the lives of the saints a multitude of examples of the manner in which people have attempted to follow the call to discipleship that is Christian morality.

Finally, nobody concerned with the seriousness of the challenge facing schools to promote moral maturity could be unaware of the importance of the contemporary challenge posed to the promotion of societal and religious values by the rise of a relativist and/or subjectivist ethos. In this context, the teaching of the broad variety of moral codes will have to be done in a manner that draws students' attention to the importance of acknowledging the objective nature of morality as opposed to accepting uncritically either a relativist or a subjectivist standpoint. In the light of the need to critique an exaggerated acceptance of pluralism, there is also a need to acknowledge that not all theories are equally valid, and moral decision-making is not simply a matter of applying one's own personal preference.

What is proposed in these commentaries?

Given the breadth and scope of the Syllabus it is undoubtedly true that teachers will have to attend to the wide variety of sections in the Syllabus which demand a breadth of knowledge that some may find a little daunting. Even though it is not envisaged that teachers would attempt to teach all ten sections of the Syllabus to any one group of students, nevertheless, the Syllabus will make demands upon teachers that can only be met if there are support services in place. For example, apart from the need to ensure the publishing of good quality teaching and learning resources, the schools themselves will need to ensure that appropriate resources – books, CDs, internet and videos – are provided. Finally, teachers will need to be provided with appropriate in-service training. It is to furthering this goal of providing good quality teaching and learning resources that the present series of volumes is addressed.

The eleven volumes in this series of commentaries comprise an introductory volume (already published, *Willingly To School*) that reflects upon the challenge of RE as an examination subject, along with ten other volumes that mirror the ten sections in the Syllabus. These commentaries on the Syllabus have been published to address the critical issue of the need to provide resources for the teaching of the Syllabus that are both academically rigorous and yet accessible to the educated general reader. Although primarily addressed to both specialist and general teachers of religion and third-level students studying to be religion teachers, the commentaries will be accessible to parents of Leaving Certificate pupils and, in addition, it is to be hoped that they will provide an important focus for adults in parish-based or other religious education or theology programmes. In the light of this focus, each of the volumes is structured in order to closely reflect the content of the Syllabus and its order of presentation. Furthermore, they are written in clear, easily accessible language and each includes an explanation of new theological and philosophical perspectives.

The volumes offered in this series are as follows

Patrick M. Devitt:	*Willingly to School: Religious Education as an Examination Subject*
Eoin G. Cassidy:	*The Search for Meaning and Values*
Thomas Norris and Brendan Leahy:	*Christianity: Origins and Contemporary Expressions*
Philip Barnes:	*World Religions*
Patrick Hannon:	*Moral Decision Making*
Sandra Cullen:	*Religion and Gender*
John Murray:	*Issues of Justice and Peace*
Christopher O'Donnell:	*Worship, Prayer and Ritual*
Benedict Hegarty:	*The Bible: Literature and Sacred Text*
John Walsh:	*Religion: The Irish Experience*
Fachtna McCarthy and Joseph McCann:	*Religion and Science*

Thanks are due to the generosity of our contributors who so readily agreed to write a commentary on each of the sections in the new Leaving Certificate Syllabus. Each of them brings to their commentary both academic expertise and a wealth of experience in the teaching of their particular area. In the light of this, one should not underestimate the contribution that they will make to the work of preparing teachers for this challenging project. Thanks are also due to our publishers, Veritas. Their unfailing encouragement and practical support has been of inestimable value to us and has ensured that these volumes saw the light of day. Finally, we hope that you the reader will find each of these commentaries helpful as you negotiate the paths of a new and challenging syllabus.

Eoin G. Cassidy
Patrick M. Devitt
Series Editors

Preface

Though somewhat distant in time, a period as a teacher of religion at second level has left various memories with me, one of which is that the busy teacher is unlikely to have time for a great deal of reading around the programme. This piece of seeming common sense, however, contends in my mind with another piece of common sense, which is that we never achieve a grasp of any subject without serious reflection of our own; and this won't come easily to the reader of just one book.

Some readers will doubtless regard this as proof only that one's exposure to teaching religion at post-primary level was too long ago and far too brief. But it will perhaps help to explain why I thought the most useful approach might be to allow the book to develop according to what seems the natural logic of an introductory reflection. So it doesn't follow the syllabus step by step, though it does aim to cover the ground.[1]

And, departing from a current fashion, may I suggest that it be read in its entirety at first, as a preliminary to closer and more intensive study of its parts. A closer study should be helped by the references given in the text, and especially by judicious use of the auxiliary material in the bibliography. A practical suggestion about the textbooks in both moral theology and moral philosophy: the reader might have a look through a selection of each in order to see which appeals most. Each has its virtues, but a teacher's own instinct is the best guide as to which is the one for him or her.[2]

I owe many thanks to a number of people who read all or part of the text in draft: Pádraig Corkery, Amelia Fleming, Dermot Lane, Vincent MacNamara, Lisa Maye, Suzanne Mulligan, Caroline Renehan, Paul Tighe, and Josette Zammit-Mangion. Special thanks to Damien Keown, Professor of Buddhist Ethics at Goldsmiths College, University of London, for help concerning Buddhist references and reading materials, and to Anthony O'Mahoney SJ, Director of Research at the Centre for Inter-religious Dialogue, Heythrop College, University of London, for similar assistance concerning Islam. Elma Byrne proofed the manuscript with customary diligence and accuracy. Thanks also to the series editors and the readers at Veritas. All the help so readily given has undoubtedly resulted in an improved text, though as usual no-one but the author can be blamed for remaining defects. The book was completed while I was a Visiting Fellow at St Edmund's College, Cambridge, during the Lent and Easter Terms 2004, and I thank the Master and Fellows for electing me into the Fellowship.

Finally, I wish to acknowledge the contribution of first-year students in moral theology at Maynooth during the past three decades or so (I hope they're not too surprised), and of participants in extra-mural religion courses throughout the country during the same period. At least those of them who are teachers will by now know that teaching teaches you.

Notes
1   A guide to which chapters cover the various sections of the syllabus can be found on p.28.
2   Although it was written as a resource for teachers of the new Leaving Certificate religion course I hope that the book may be useful to other readers also.

Introduction

Introduction

This book is an extended reflection on the dimension of our experience to which we give the name morality. The question 'what is morality?' will itself be a major theme, but we can say provisionally now that it is about how we relate to other people and to the world around us. We are of course already engaged in so relating, but it may be somewhat in the manner of the man in Molière's play who found that he spoke prose all his life without knowing it. That is, we are, all our lives and every day, making moral decisions for good or ill, though we may not up to now have reflected much on the experience. So what we are embarking upon is not some esoteric study but only a reflective look at an experience which is familiar.

It is possible to think about morality from various standpoints, and it is, therefore, studied in a variety of disciplines, for example, psychology, sociology, anthropology, each of which views it in terms of the particular discipline's own presuppositions and methodologies and objectives, and each of which sheds important light. But it is possible also to think about it in a way which focuses on the essence of the experience, on what characterises it and distinguishes it from other (sometimes apparently similar) experiences, and on how it might be interpreted in terms of human experience generally. It is possible, that is, to think about it 'philosophically', to try to see where it fits into the general scheme of things.

Our own reflection takes place in the light of Christian beliefs about humanity and human destiny, which means it is an exercise in Christian moral theology. Morality might be studied without reference to religious belief, as it is in moral philosophy, but religions generally have something to say about morality, and usually they undertake to teach something of 'the good life', of how we ought to live. Christianity, like the other major world religions, proposes to its followers a way of life, and Christian religious faith has a bearing upon the moral life; moral theology investigates how and to what extent this is so.

In moral theology it is usual to distinguish between *fundamental* or *general* moral theology on the one hand, and *special* or *particular* or *applied* on the other. The names speak for themselves. For example, fundamental moral theology examines concepts and doctrines which underlie the whole enterprise of Christian ethics; special moral theology looks at particular areas such as justice, bioethics, sexual ethics, ethics and communications. These special topics are dealt with in other books in the *Into the Classroom* series; this one's concern, however, is with fundamentals: what morality is, how we make moral judgments, where Christian faith comes in, and so on.

The Christian tradition from which this reflection starts is the Roman Catholic one, but I hope it will emerge that this does not mean entrapment in what is sometimes called a 'sectarian' view. For it is a tenet of Catholic moral theology itself that morality is a feature of common human experience and that its essential demands are discoverable by reason. And for all that there are differences between the Christian traditions, and between Christian and other religious and non-religious views, there is also a great deal in common.

It will then, perhaps, not be so surprising that for almost half of the book, the language is largely secular. The nature of morality, the process of making moral judgements, the conditions for development toward moral maturity – all of these are explored without the use of specifically Christian terminology or concepts. Only when this has been done to its limit is the dimension of Christian faith invoked and investigated.[1]

But this may yet strike some readers as artificial, since most people likely to use the book will have received their ideas about morality along with or as part of their Christian faith. And their behaviour will have been moulded by Christian ideas about what it is to be human, and what it takes to live well in the world. Why not from the outset speak of morality in explicitly Christian terms? Why not see it from the outset in the interpretive framework which Christian beliefs supply? A fuller answer to these questions should emerge as we go along, but the following may be said for now.

First, as mentioned a moment ago, it is a datum of Catholic theology itself – of mainline Christian tradition[2] in fact – that morality is a common human experience of which much may be said without recourse to what is made of it by Christian theology. And, second, it will be important for Christians to make common cause with people of other faiths and of none, in the common pursuit of justice and peace in our world; and in this enterprise there is an obvious advantage in a common language. Third, granted that there are many for whom religious concepts and terminology mean little or nothing, it is well to be able to speak of morality in secular terms. Finally, neither religion nor morality is helped by some of the connections which are made between them, and the prospect for an appropriate view of their relationships is improved if they can be seen in a way which gives each its due weight.

And so, **chapters one** and **two** consider the core of the experience that we call morality. This is a recognition that in the way we relate to each other and to the world around us there is 'good' and 'bad', 'right and 'wrong', and, concomitantly, a sense

of obligation to do what is right and good and to avoid what is
bad and wrong. What is meant by these terms, and where does
the sense of obligation come from? There are things that we
name as good – a good day, for example, or a good song or
game or piece of art – but about which we don't speak of
obligation. Or we might speak of being obliged by the law or
by etiquette to do or refrain from something, and yet we might
want to say that these aren't matters of morality. What
distinguishes the experiences we call 'moral' from those which
might look like morality, but are not?

We shall soon advert also to the fact that when we speak of
what is morally good or bad we refer not just to *acts* (or
omissions) but also to *states of affairs*, as when we criticise a
socio-political situation for being racially discriminatory. More
significantly perhaps, we think also of 'inner' realities such as
motivation, intention, attitude and disposition. We see
someone do what on the outside seems a good act, such as
helping someone in need, but we recognise that the moral
value of the act may be impaired by a bad attitude
(condescension, say) or motive (to impress) or intention (to
create in the other a feeling of dependence).

So being moral is not just a matter of doing or refraining
from certain kinds of acts; it involves also those inner realities.
And so we speak of the moral life not just in terms of right and
wrong actions but also in terms of the mentality behind our
actions; and also of underlying patterns of behaviour or traits
of character, expressed in what we do but also influencing what
we do. We speak, in other words, of virtues and vices, more or
less settled states out of which we behave, and which our
behaviour reinforces. And we shall be trying to find a
description of morality which makes due room for each of
these dimensions.

Making moral judgments is at the heart of the matter, and
chapter three examines what is involved in this. *Conscience* is
the term given to that aspect of our make-up whose concern is

with making such judgments. What exactly is this 'aspect'? Are we born with it? How may it develop? What is meant by saying that we must follow our conscience? Is everything down to what we 'feel' about things, or are there principles which we have to have in mind, and which guide or shape our behaviour?

And what do we do when presented with a moral dilemma? Most people would agree that, for example, we ought to keep confidences, and the value of keeping confidences can be shown without much difficulty. But what if keeping a confidence means telling a lie? Or what, to take a particular application, is to become of the obligation of a doctor not to disclose information about a patient's condition if to keep confidence will result in a HIV patient's infecting a partner? And are there some actions which may never be done, no matter how acute a dilemma? Catholic moral theology offers approaches to such questions, and these will be the subject of **chapter four**.

If we look at our own experience we can see fairly easily that an important aspect of our theme is the question of *becoming* moral. The concept of becoming is in this context apt in several ways. First, it is obvious that we have to *learn* morality, to learn what morality requires, and how to live up to its requirements. A child learns right and wrong, is guided toward certain ways of behaving, gradually comes to learn the reasons for behaving thus, and gradually acquires *knowledge* of the sort of conduct that is good or bad. But we have to learn also the *practice* of virtue, and our progress is never linear. What are we to make of the fact that for all that we may know what is right, and for all that we try to live a good life, we sometimes fail? Is moral failure always – or ever – our fault? Becoming moral is the subject of **chapter five**.

So much for morality as a fact of human experience generally, that is, as something which is found among human beings simply by virtue of their being human, and which may be spoken of without reference to religion. Where then does religion come in? We consider this in a general way in **chapter six**. One way of approaching an answer is to say that how we choose to relate to people depends on what we make of them, and what we make of them depends in the end on what we make of life. And what we make of life may be called our vision of life, the picture which we have of what it means to be a human being in the world.

The sense of this may be seen when we consider possible implications of a well-known dictum of the philosopher Thomas Hobbes, who said that human life was 'solitary, poor, nasty, brutish and short'. Consider how we might behave if we truly believed that life is like that. We should, one can imagine, be pretty pessimistic about what to expect from our fellow humans, and therefore defensive in our relationships with them – or perhaps offensive, on the basis that the best form of defence is attack. We would be likely to be competitive, and ruthless in the way in which we strove to get our way and to prevent others from getting theirs. It could be expected that qualities such as compassion, kindness or mercy would find little place in our make-up.

The point is that our picture or vision of life is what shapes our conduct of our lives, and this is always so, even if the lineaments of the picture are not always explicit or present to our consciousness. The picture which many people have of life is a religious one, and for the moment it will do to think of this simply as involving the belief that there is a God, however this God may be conceived. But of course the question how this God is conceived is an important one: consider the difference between a view which sees God as providential and loving, and one for whom the foremost qualities of God are of a being who is stern and vengeful, quick to anger and slow to love.

It is at this level, at the level of providing a vision of life in the light of which we may lead our lives, that religion is most fundamentally related to morality. True, religions characteristically summon their followers to a particular way of life, a particular morality. And, like its parent Judaism, Christianity recognises no separation between love of God and love of neighbour, and it calls on its adherents to love one another as Jesus loved. But that call makes sense only when understood against the larger background of the religious message of Jesus, that part of his message and mission which tells of God and of God's plan for humans and for the rest of creation.

What is the religious message of Jesus, and how does his moral teaching relate to it? To answer this, one must look in the first place at the Bible, the source par excellence of all thinking about the meaning of the message of Christianity. **Chapter seven** considers what might be involved in this, and in particular it examines the way in which the Bible may illuminate the Christian's quest for a path lit by faith in Jesus Christ. Jesus was not in the first place a teacher of morality, though he did teach things about morality. And when you recall that what he says and exemplifies is that God is love, it is not strange that he should also say that the first commandment was love of God and neighbour, for love invites love.

It is no doubt one thing to acknowledge that the greatest commandment is the love commandment but quite another to say what the love commandment means. And a central part of our own concern here will be with that question, to be faced in **chapters eight and nine**. Naturally, what the bible has to say about this will be critical, and what it has to say will not be a matter just of the teaching of Jesus but also of how he lived, and of the impact of the gospel message upon the young churches.

But we shall find that to insist upon the primacy of the love commandment does not relieve us of the task of working out the concrete requirements of that command, in all of the situations in which we find ourselves and in every epoch of history. Which is to say that espousal of the love commandment is espousal of the common ethical task of discovering the right way to behave. Love is not a vague benevolence, but an attitude of the heart which impels us to find and do what is best in service of our fellows and of our world. And the finding involves using our heads, using reason, imagination, and empathy – discerning and judging what is best done here and now.

Right discernment presupposes not only a grasp of moral principles and a skill in their application but also an openness to 'the good'. For a religious person this will mean an openness to God, a conscious and consciously cultivated relationship with the ultimate ground of being and of the good. This means that Christian moral living bespeaks a *spirituality* which includes prayer and worship, for it is in prayer and worship that the Christian's relationship with God is cultivated. In mainline Christian theology spirituality is Christ-centred and it is also to a greater or lesser extent 'sacramental', and in **chapter ten** we shall see something of what this entails; and it will be clear yet again that one cannot claim to love the God of Jesus Christ without being fully committed to love of the fellow human being.

Chapter eleven offers an account of the relationships between morality and law, something which may require explanation. For it will have already been pointed out that morality and law are not at all the same thing, and that harm has sometimes been done through confusing them; and it might be thought that to re-introduce law at the conclusion of our study, is to give it a false importance and to risk the confusion we have been trying to avoid.

But it seems important to tease out the detail at more length, and precisely so as to minimise the scope for confusion. For law and morality are of course interconnected and interdependent, and indeed in some respects they resemble each other; and there are times when it is easy to confuse them, sometimes with unhappy results for morality. So this short reflection on what morality means may helpfully be brought to a conclusion by comparing and contrasting it with law, and by looking at two central questions in particular – whether there is a moral obligation to obey the law, and whether it is the law's business to enforce or promote morals. This latter question has of course added significance in a society in which there is a 'pluralism' of religious and moral belief and practice, and it will allow us to give some consideration to the concept of a 'common good' (**chapter twelve**).

A word about some decisions which have had to be made, and questions which may already have suggested themselves to the reader. Someone teaching the new syllabus will have to deal with the morality of other religions besides the Christian (see Syllabus Section 2.1); why are other moralities mentioned here only in passing? There are two reasons. First, I think it is possible to look appreciatively at the moralities of other religions only when one has thoroughly understood one's own; and, second, it would be absurd to think that justice is done to any vision of morality by way of a short summary in a short book. A reader who is interested in acquiring an understanding of the subtle and complex ways of the other major faiths will be helped, I hope, by the reading suggested for each.

Something similar arises in relation to *philosophical theories* of morality (see Syllabus Section 3.2). Catholic moral theology does not tie itself to any particular ethical theory, yet it is plain that its view of morality excludes some of them, and finds others more or less congenial. What these are will emerge as we go along, and sometimes it will be useful to give a rough summary of their main tenets. But there can be no question of a full account, if only for the reason that in the case of the main theories there isn't just one version but several, and anything short of an extended treatment must involve excessive simplification. Again I hope that the suggested reading will afford entry to a proper study.

Finally, I have been conscious that the book's potential readership includes both people who have already studied moral theology (or moral philosophy) and people who haven't.

Morality and the moral life are not mysterious, and in general it should be possible to think and talk about them in plain language. But there is an irreducible technical vocabulary, and there are some theoretical issues which cannot be overlooked. I hope that in trying to strike the right note, this book neither bores the already knowledgeable nor leaves the beginner adrift.

To facilitate the work of teachers, I outline below the manner in which I address the topics covered in the Leaving Certificate Religious Education Syllabus. The list of chapters within brackets indicates the places at which these are directly or indirectly discussed.

The Religious Education Syllabus

Part One, entitled *Thinking about Morality*, has three sub-sections:
1.1   The Meaning of Morality (chapter 1)
1.2   Why be Moral? (chapter 2)
1.3   The Common Good and Individual Rights (chapters 11 and 12)

Part Two, entitled *Morality and Religion*, has three sub-sections:
2.1   The Relationship between Morality and Religion (chapter 6)
2.2   Morality and the Christian Tradition (chapters 7, 8, 9, and 10)
2.3   Religious Perspectives on Moral Failure (the last part of chapter 5)

Part Three, entitled *Moral Principles and Theories*, has two sub-sections:
3.1   Morality in a Pluralist Society (chapters 11 and 12)
3.2   Moral Theories in Action (parts of chapters 2 and 3)

Part Four, entitled *Moral Development*, has three sub-sections:
4.1   Towards Moral Maturity (chapter 5)
4.2   Conscience (chapters 3, 4, 5)
4.3   Decision-Making in Action.

Notes

1   This is also of course, in broad terms, the methodology of the Leaving Certificate Religion syllabus.

2   I use this expression here and later in reference to Christian theology which relies upon reason and human experience – and to a greater or lesser extent, church tradition – as well as on biblical revelation, especially in addressing concrete ethical issues. Within this general approach there is some variety as to the relative weight accorded the various ingredients, as is suggested by the (simplistic) contrast sometimes made between Christian 'natural law' and 'evangelical' ethics. The most radical alternative is what is usually called biblical fundamentalism, an approach which almost invariably treats biblical material literally. It is fair to say that the broader approach has always been the dominant Christian tradition.

I

What Being Moral Means

If you ask someone what being moral means, the reply is likely to be along the lines of one of the following: 'doing what's right and avoiding what's wrong', 'doing good and avoiding evil', 'keeping the moral law', 'acting according to conscience' – or, if the person is religious, 'keeping the Commandments', or 'keeping God's law', or perhaps 'following Jesus'. And if you press the question it will emerge that at the core of the experience which we call morality is, first, recognition of a *distinction* between right and wrong, good and evil, and, second, a *sense of obligation* to do what is good and right, and to avoid what is evil and wrong.

Recognition of such a distinction and the accompanying sense of obligation are universal. People may differ concerning *what* is right or wrong, as when some consider euthanasia or capital punishment to be morally permissible while for others these are wrong because they are the deliberate taking of a human life. People differ also as to the *nature and source of the obligation* in question, some believing it to be in a law of God, others believing it to be a trait of our nature which impels us towards what will ensure our happiness or at least our survival. Later we shall have to explore some of these differences, but for now it is enough to notice that the belief *that* there is a right and wrong, and that we *ought* to do what is right, is normally and generally found, and people who lack a sense of the distinction and obligation are thought to suffer from a psychopathology.

Moral imperatives
But we use the terms 'right' and 'wrong' and 'good' and 'bad' and 'ought' in various contexts, and it requires little reflection to see that the words don't carry the same weight in each of the contexts in which they may occur. Consider for example the following propositions:

- You ought to respect human life
- You ought to read Shakespeare
- You ought to drive on the left hand side of the road
- You ought to use a fish-knife

Each of these is in imperative form, each injuncts us to an attitude or action or activity, each intimates some kind of obligation. But is the *ought* of the same weight in each case?[1]

One way of approaching this is to ask about the significance of what is enjoined in each – the question of whether the imperatives are equally important. Intuitively we should ascribe greater importance to the first and the third, somewhat less to the second, and not a lot to the fourth. If asked about this line of preference we should probably respond in terms of the importance of each for 'life' or 'living' or some such. We are also likely to say of the injunction to read Shakespeare or – if we give it much credence at all – the injunction to use a fish-knife, that in these cases 'it all depends'.

Of course we ought to read Shakespeare *if* we are following a course in which his plays are on the syllabus, or if in any case we want to acquaint ourselves with the achievements of English literature. Of course we ought to use a fish-knife *if* one has been provided by a punctilious host or hostess; not to do so would betray some lack of table etiquette, and to refuse to do so would at the least seem ungracious. Reading Shakespeare is the relatively more important pursuit, failure to use a fish-knife is not a matter of great moment; and any obligation which might arise in either case is a *conditional* one.

Not so with the imperative 'you ought to respect human life'. We have already remarked that the subject matter of this is more serious – the injunction has to do with life or living in a quite fundamental way. We shall see later something of what respect for life might mean, but for now we can take it that 'respect' in general terms means having regard for, being constructive about, not making little of, not harming, above all not destroying. And it's plain that lack of respect for human life strikes at the root of everything we consider important about human living.

Of this first imperative, then, we can say that it holds *unconditionally* – *absolutely*, if you like – because it is fundamental to any kind of human well-being. But can we say the same about the third – you ought to drive on the left? Ordinarily it will be for us a derivative of the first, or based on it, for it is intimately connected to safety on the roads and so to the protection or non-endangering of people's lives. But it is not unconditional, for of course it doesn't hold in most of continental Europe nor in the United States, to mention but two large territories in which it is not the law. Nor would one insist on driving on the left if to do so meant driving over someone who had fallen on the road. So a topic arises which we shall have to examine at some length later, for although in this and other matters morality and the law intersect, they are separable aspects of our experience, and the differences between them are important.

We might summarise the foregoing by saying that as we live life we meet various kinds of imperatives and obligations, some relatively trivial as to content and weight, some more important. The important ones bear upon important aspects of human living, that is they have to do with what we value most about life because they are connected with the enhancement of our existence. In addition, to respect for life, one might add regard for other rights, such as the right to a good name or a fair wage; or one might say such things as we ought to be just and truthful and faithful and compassionate. In each case we should be saying that 'virtues' or traits or qualities such as these, and the actions to which they give rise, are what make for our flourishing as human persons.

But we need to notice one other feature of the imperatives just examined, which is that they all have to do with our relationships with each other and with the world around us. And here we hit upon a critical aspect of our existence as humans, which is that we are relational beings, and we cannot adequately be understood if this is lost sight of. We come into the world as the fruit of the relationship of our parents, and even for survival we need from the outset to be in some kind of sustaining relationship with another. In normal circumstances a child is in a dependent relationship first to its mother, and he or she comes to maturity in a network of other relationships which contribute to nurturing and education in a complex variety of ways.

At first our relationships are non-reflective, some of them even unconscious: spontaneously we just *are* – children or sisters or brothers or pupils or friends, or a doctor's patients or a hairdresser's customers. But as we grow in self-awareness we become aware of our relationships, and we become aware of being able to make some choices in their regard. I cannot change the fact that I am a child of X and Y, but I find that I have some control over the way in which I behave towards them. I cannot avoid being in the relationship of classmate to Z, but I can choose whether or not I want Z for a friend.

Understanding, choice and responsibility
These characteristics of the human being, awareness (more exactly, understanding) and a capacity for choice, are the

foundation of morality. Understanding tells us something about the way the world is, and our capacity for choice allows us to decide how we are going to conduct ourselves in it. A more familiar way of putting this is to say that humans are knowing and free, and that their knowledge and freedom are the basis for morality. An even more familiar account is that it's because we possess intellect and will that we can distinguish and choose between right and wrong.

Not that our knowledge is often full and clear, or our freedom ever absolutely pure. We can forget, make mistakes, are sometimes ignorant of truth; and sometimes our judgment is clouded by excess of emotion, or by factors deep in our psychology of which we may not even be conscious. Our freedom is always bounded by our knowledge, and it may be trammelled too by compulsions and fears and other stirrings of the psyche, including, again, forces within us of which we may not even be aware.[2]

Our knowledge and our freedom are invariably affected also by our environment. This may be seen in an obvious way when we look at, say, a child from a deprived urban setting. The child may not know right from wrong simply because he or she may never have been taught, either at home or at school (for of course these are where moral rules and values are normally mainly learned). Or they may have been taught in a nominal sense but the values or rules may not have registered, perhaps because of a discrepancy between what they hear and what they see others do. Or indeed what has been taught may have registered, but a social pressure seems nevertheless to drive them to steal or maim or take drugs.

This kind of illustration of the influence of the environment is commonplace, but we needn't think that environmental or peer pressure is confined to those whom we think of as 'deprived'. Moral sensibility may be imperilled also in settings which we usually think of as 'privileged': as when the context in which I live precludes my ever seeing dole-queues or the signs of homelessness, and I remain untroubled by the inequities in our society of which these are symptoms. Any of us might be blinded by the prejudices of our background so that we are deprived of the capacity to recognise and respond to certain kinds of good and evil.

Yet normally we have sufficient knowledge and capacity for choice to be able in some fashion to direct and shape our lives. The recognition that we are always influenced by the make-up or our environment has not persuaded people to abandon the language of praise or blame, or to cease to try to change our ways, or encourage others to change theirs. This is to say that people generally hold on to the idea of moral *responsibility* – to the idea that we are *able* to make something of ourselves and our world, and that we are *answerable* for what we make of ourselves and how.

So the dimension of experience which we call morality is founded on our capacity to know and to choose; these characteristics of the human are what enable us to choose how we are to relate to other people and to our world. And at this stage we might hazard a description of morality as the art of right relationship with each other and with the world around us.[3] The choice of the word 'art' may at first be puzzling, and I shall explain it in due course. But first we might take a closer look at the word 'right', and the notion that there is a right and a wrong way of relating.

Right or wrong, good or bad?
Right and wrong in terms of what? We may for the moment think of right as indicating conformity with a rule: with being just, for example, as required by a rule that we ought to be just; or giving help to someone in need, in accordance with the principle that we ought to help the needy; or refraining from stealing, according to the precept that we ought not to steal. But why these rules or principles or precepts, or where did they come from, and why should we conform to them?

We might answer this by reflecting that another way of putting the foregoing is that it's 'good' to be just, or to help those in need, and that it is 'evil' or 'bad' to steal. Speaking very strictly, the terms right and wrong, even in a moral context, are in the first place descriptive of compliance or otherwise with some standard. But inevitably there is also a suggestion of commendation or disapproval of whatever or whomever is said to be right or wrong. And with the expressions good and evil this evaluative ingredient comes into prominence: a good radio is to be prized and praised, as is a good read – or a good hurler or footballer or carpenter or parent; and a good person makes, as it were, a demand upon our regard.

A good person? It's not hard to judge whether a radio is good or bad, or a book – or indeed a singer or footballer or student. For it is not difficult to find criteria by which these judgments may be made, even if people sometimes disagree as to the precise criteria, or on how they are to be ranked, or how exactly applied. But a good person? Following a classical philosophical tradition and adapting the Oxford English Dictionary we can say that we call a thing good when it is what it was called to be. So a person is good when she or he is what he or she is *called* to be. 'Call' is figurative; a religious person may think here of the call of God, but the expression need mean no more than that a particular way of being or acting is according to our nature.

And what is that? Several answers are possible. If what characterises the human person are the twin gifts of reason and freedom, we are what we are called to be when we exercise our freedom rationally. And that is indeed an apt description of what being moral means. But it is abstract and general, and people may be attracted by a somewhat warmer way of putting it; and more than one religious or philosophical tradition would be happy with the proposition that human beings are called to love.

Love is a troublesome word, its meaning confused in the variety of its usage. A child loves ice-cream as well as his parents, a whole generation loved the Rolling Stones, Dante loved Beatrice, Diarmuid loved Gráinne, Hamlet loved Ophelia, and Don Juan (it seems) loved many women. C.S. Lewis wrote a book called *The Four Loves*, from which it may be seen that even when we use the word aptly we may be talking of different forms. But there is at least the residue of a core meaning, and for present purposes we can say that love means wishing people well and doing them good.

So the good person is one who loves. But this is too general, it tells us nothing about how we ought in practice to behave, and we need immediately to give it concrete content. We could say that to love is to appreciate another, to have regard (in more than one sense); and to express this appreciation and regard in our dispositions and attitudes and intentions and actions. We should therefore acknowledge the dignity of others, respect their life and person, aim to do them good, be just and truthful, don't steal from them or take away their good name, and refrain from harming them in any way.

These are some of the 'rules' of morality, and they follow from the nature of the enterprise, and the nature of the enterprise is determined by our nature as human beings. Humans are called to love, and the 'precepts' or 'commandments' which are a feature of all moral systems are simply statements of a standard or test of loving. Later we shall have to see how the various kinds of principle and rule can help us achieve moral truth. Meanwhile we must ask the question, why be moral?

Notes

1   We should not be misled by the colloquialism by which 'ought' is
     often understood as meaning 'it would be a good idea', as when
     someone says you ought to take an umbrella because it's likely to
     rain. In the language of ethical discourse 'ought' signifies
     obligation.

2   Connections between psychology and morality (and spirituality)
     are explored in Vincent MacNamara, *New Life for Old*, Dublin, 2004.

3   'Love thy neighbour as thyself' is a familiar expression of the
     central moral imperative of Christianity. Right relationship with
     other people and with our world presupposes right relationship
     with oneself.

2

Why be Moral?

Earlier when we asked ourselves where moral rules come from we saw that in the most obvious sense they come from the tradition of the community. Now, again obviously, we can see that the demand that we keep the rules comes from the community, concretely mediated through parents, teachers, peers, society's laws and institutions. But where did the community get the rules, and why should it ask us to keep them? It's worth pursuing these questions a little. One of the reasons why people – especially the young – resist moral rules is that they reject the authority of whomever they perceive to be imposing them.

Some readers may be surprised that I do not now adduce God as the author of moral rules – what about the Ten Commandments? The Sermon on the Mount? – and God's will as the basis of our obligation to keep them. Many people see morality in exactly this way: as God's law which must be kept because God said so, and because God will punish or reward us, depending upon the measure of our compliance. The reason I do not adduce God as the author of the rules of morality is that God is not their author *in this sense* at all. And harm is done both to our notion of God and to our grasp of morality when we conceive God's connection with morality in this way. We shall have to see more of this later.

Natural law

But where *do* the rules come from, and why obey them? Their author is the human mind, reflecting on human experience, discovering what is or is not fit living for a creature with a human nature. This discovery is always in process, for there is no end to change in the conditions of our living, and the change forces us to a ceaseless search for the right way for humans to live. There are of course some constants: we are body-spirits, with minds and hearts and will – rational and free, as the philosophers have it. We are sexual beings with an instinct for the reproduction of our kind. We need food, clothing and shelter. We need also to search for the 'truth' of things, to comprehend ourselves and our world. And these constants generate certain general requirements of human flourishing – which is another way of saying that the general requirements of morality do not change. But their concrete application varies, and we are never freed from the quest for the right way.

I have used the expression 'human flourishing' in reference to the point of being moral; an older expression is 'fulfilment', older still (but perhaps misleading) the word 'happiness'. What is in question is the idea that the point of anything is that it should *be* in the way which best suits the kind of thing it is: that things always aim at the 'perfection' of whatever their nature is. And the perfection of human nature is in the direction of rational choice – or of loving, if you prefer that way of putting it. Humans flourish inasmuch as they exercise their freedom according to the claims of reality, the claims of their own nature and the nature of things generally, or again, more warmly, when they truly love.

The foregoing is no more than a fairly standard account of what mainline Christian theology has meant by the doctrine of natural law. And we shall see that the concept is enhanced, though not in substance altered, in the light of Christian beliefs about ultimate human destiny. There have been theological

objections to it: notably the Lutheran one that it makes too
much of both nature and reason, ignoring the radical damage
to humanity that is expressed in the notion of the Fall. Other
critics think that there are so many problems about the idea of
a 'law of nature', especially when it purports to describe
unvarying moral demands, that it is not now seriously
serviceable as an account of the basis of morality. Yet the
essential ingredients of the doctrine have proved difficult to
dispense with and it remains central, albeit in newer versions –
and sometimes in disguise – in much Christian moral theology
still.[1]

Survival or more?

Of course some will say that the point of being moral is simply
survival: that the demands of morality originated and have
their justification in the concrete conditions of the persistence
of individuals and of the species. But does this accord with our
experience? It may well be that historically the first perceptions
of, say, the value of life were self-interested, or that what came
to be called the Golden Rule was at first no more than the
insight that it is expedient to live and let live. And no doubt we
sometimes do what is right from self-interest rather than from
nobler motives. But we are never content for long with this
version of things. We are not content with mere survival but
are drawn to a certain 'quality' in our living. In the context of
our relationships that quality includes attitudes such as
gentleness and compassion and unselfishness. It calls on us
sometimes to turn the other cheek or go the second mile; and
it asks some to lay down their life for their friend. Such
manifestations of the flourishing of humanity are not
explicable merely in terms of survival.

Moral rules come to us out of the tradition of the
community, but their ultimate origin is in the race's attempt to
make sense of its experience; or, if you like, in human reason
reflecting on human nature. And we ought therefore to obey

the rules not just as it were on the say-so of the community or
its authorities, but because and to the extent that they indicate
the way of human flourishing. The answer to the question,
why be moral? is not because society or the Church or even
God requires it, but that it is through being moral that we
become truly human.

This account of the origin of morality and the basis of
moral obligation is intelligible to people other than religious
believers, and in discussion with people who are not believers it
is obviously preferable to an account couched in religious
language. But that is not its only value, and at least as important
is the fact that it gives morality its own independent weight.
When moral right and wrong are seen as based exclusively on a
command of God they are in danger of being seen as merely
extrinsically imposed, and our grasp of morality's significance
is thereby impoverished. Its significance for the flourishing of
our nature is then likely to be obscured, and it is seen as alien
rather than as congenial to us. Consequently, we submit to (or
resist) its claims, not in understanding and freedom but more or
less blindly, in a way best described as infantile. We shall discuss
this more in due course.

An art?
A description of morality offered in the preceding chapter
spoke of it as an 'art', and it is time now to explain why. The
word is apposite for it is suggestive at several levels. Its most
basic sense is of a skill which comes from knowledge and
practice,[2] and we have seen enough to appreciate how morality
might be described as an art in this sense. Plainly it requires a
knowledge, an ensemble of notions and values and principles
which express in the concrete the requirements of the good life.
The good life, however, is to be *lived*, not just known or
appreciated in the abstract. Moral knowledge is for putting into
practice, and the practice both expresses and reinforces our ideas
about how we are meant to live.

The word 'art' is suggestive in another way, for it also intimates a performance or achievement which is more than the simple application of a rule. There are principles of musical composition for example, but the art of Beethoven is more than his observance of these rules. One could say, I suppose, that among the things which make us regard him as a great composer is the way in which he 'works with' the rules, fashioning in music his vision. Vision in this context is not (if it ever is) something of the mind only; music too is, as Wordsworth in 'Tintern Abbey' said of poetry, felt in the blood and felt along the heart. And as in poetry or music, moral sensibility includes an engagement of the feelings and of the imagination which allows us to 'see into the life of things'.

Justice, as Aristotle said, is not merely the doing of just actions but the doing of them in the way of the just person.[3] That means behaving out of a right intention and motive and attitude, and a general disposition to justice. And a disposition to justice or any other form of goodness, translated into practice, leads to a certain ease of performance. Someone who possesses the appropriate 'art' will be observed to play golf or to sing or paint with a kind of fluency. And so it is with morals: disposition translates into habit, and habit tends toward facility, and we develop a 'style'. In this sense too, therefore, we might speak of an art of good living.

There is a fourth reason for conceiving of good living as an art. It is that the best achievements of the artist are sometimes experienced by him or her (and perceived by others) as somehow 'given', as it were, from outside. People speak of being 'taken over', 'possessed', 'inspired', so that their performance – as painter, actor, footballer – exceeds what they had thought to be their potential. This too may happen in the moral life when we appear to transcend ourselves, to be more courageous or loving or truthful than is 'natural' for us; and we may aptly speak of having been 'gifted'. The religious person will think of the concept of grace, which suggests the notion of a 'gift from God' that empowers and enhances us.

Notes

1   It is also, of course, an antecedent of the concept of human rights, the idea that people have entitlements in virtue solely of their being human; and it is interesting to note that an element in the stimulus to renewed interest in natural law theory in recent times is a search for the basis of human rights.

The topic of natural law will arise again in chapter eleven – on morality and law – and mention will be made of what has become a classic introductory text, A.P. d'Entreve's *Natural Law*. Meanwhile, a good short introduction to modern thinking on natural law is in Donal Harrington, *What Is Morality?*, Dublin, 1996, 95ff.

2   *Shorter Oxford English Dictionary*, 3rd edition.

3   *Nicomachean Ethics*, Book 2, J.A.K Thomson (trans.), Harmondsworth, 1966. A very useful account of Aristotle's ethics is Gerard J. Hughes, *Aristotle on Ethics*, London/New York, 2001.

3

Making Moral Decisions

If we are to choose between right and wrong we need to be able to distinguish between them, and the capacity to do this resides in the conscience. We sometimes speak metaphorically of conscience, as when at school we were told that it is 'a little voice inside me that tells me right from wrong', or when at the Second Vatican Council it was called 'the most secret core and sanctuary' of the person where one is alone with God. These metaphors have their uses but they may also mislead, and they mislead if they give the impression that conscience is some sort of faculty or power distinct from our general power of understanding.

For moral consciousness, consciousness of a difference between right and wrong, and of an obligation to do what is right and avoid the wrong, is an aspect of consciousness generally. And we achieve moral knowledge in broadly the same way that we achieve knowledge more generally – through the ordinary educational agencies of the society into which we are born. Education is here meant in the widest sense, and it refers to the signals which from birth – perhaps before birth – a child picks up about the world, through to the processes of formal education, and including such informal processes as the influence of the various media of communication with which our world has become familiar. Later we shall see something of the way in which conscience develops.

Conscience

A pithy summary of the function of conscience is offered by the *Catechism of the Catholic Church*: 'Moral conscience, present at the heart of the person, enjoins him at the appropriate moment to do good and to avoid evil. It also judges particular choices, approving those that are good and denouncing those that are evil' (1777).[1] In a distinction which goes back to Aquinas, moral theology speaks of *synderesis*, meaning a habitual grasp of general principles, and *conscientia* which is the mechanism whereby these principles are applied to concrete situations. Of course, as we shall see later, our consciences are furnished with both general and particular principles which guide our judgment as to what is to be done or not done in the here and now.

The *Catechism*'s description of conscience's function alludes to its being 'present at the heart of the person', and this signals two important points. First, the conscience is at the core of the personality, the locus of our integrity as persons; and second, the response of conscience is not to be conceived in a narrowly intellectual way. 'Heart' is in fact the Hebrew metaphor for conscience, there being no separate word for it; and even in English the word betokens both what is deepest in the personality and what is felt and imagined as well as thought. It may be worth pursuing this a little.

Moral knowledge is not like mathematical knowledge, nor is moral judgment like the process of reaching a conclusion in algebra or geometry or arithmetic. It would be possible to set out Fermat's theorem, say, and to follow it to its conclusion without being stirred in one's soul, but the conclusion that the torture of prisoners of war is wrong is as likely to come from, or be accompanied by, a *feeling* of revulsion as it is from an inference from the principle that we shouldn't harm people. If

I draw a triangle, it hardly needs Euclid's proof to show that the sum of any two sides of it is greater than the third, and this conclusion is likely to be greeted fairly dispassionately. But if I argue that it was wrong for President Bush to go to war in Iraq, my conclusion is not going to be unaccompanied by feeling, nor will the hearer, sympathetic or otherwise, be unmoved in response.

This is one of the reasons why when offering a moral viewpoint people sometimes say 'I *feel*' (that war is wrong, that contributing to Trócaire is right). For the judgment in question is not a piece of cold ratiocination but rather, to quote Wordsworth again, 'felt in the blood and felt along the heart'. But this then may make some readers uneasy, inasmuch as it might seem to mean that moral knowledge is purely or mainly a matter of feeling, and of subjective personal feeling at that. Indeed, some people do use the expression 'I feel' (rather than 'I think' or 'I know') out of a sense of uncertainty as to the rightness of their view.

This brings us to a critical theme in any discussion of conscience, the question of what is often called freedom of conscience. It is called freedom of conscience because it refers to the claim that when it comes to making moral decisions I must make up my own mind – often thought of as a matter of being free of authority, unbound by what was done or thought before. It may be better, however, to call it the question of the primacy or ultimacy of conscience, for we shall see that it is possible to hold that the personal conscience judgment is in the end decisive without rejecting the possibility of guidance by way of principle or by way of the authority of a tradition.

Primacy of conscience

'Every conscience, whether right or wrong... obliges us in such a way that whoever acts against conscience sins'[2]: the dictum is one of Aquinas, and what it means is that one ought to follow conscience, and that it is wrong not to. Aquinas thought so strongly of this that he said that were one to believe that to abstain from fornication is wrong, one would sin by abstaining; and that if someone sincerely judged that to believe in Christ is evil, he or she would sin by embracing the Christian faith. These are arresting images as to the primacy of conscience, but of course Aquinas was not saying that fornication or lack of faith in Christ are right, and elsewhere he makes it clear that these are forbidden by God's law, of the prescriptions of which each person is required to be informed. For now, though, we should feel the full weight of this insight into the meaning of morality, and to take very seriously what it says about moral judgment's being ultimately the responsibility of the person making it.

Why should my conscience or yours be the ultimate judge, why give the conscience ultimate responsibility? Well, consider the alternative: that I would do something that I believed to be wrong, or not do what I believed to be right. In that case there would be within me a conflict between mind and will, a disharmony, a lack of integrity. It would make no *sense* to do something that I believed to be the wrong thing to do. Aquinas' own argument was similar: for him, the human is distinguished by knowledge and the power of choice, and we are being human – we are being ourselves – when we are doing what is good as reason presents it to the will. To will what one believed to be wrong would be to violate our nature.[3]

But does this mean that the judgment as to what is right or wrong is purely subjective? That nothing is either good or bad but thinking makes it so? That Adolf Hitler's policy of extermination of Jewish people and gypsies and homosexuals was, as his 'opinion', as entitled to respect as is the view that genocide is always wrong? Nowadays there is much emphasis on subjectivity and/or relativity[4] in moral judgment, and a tentativeness about taking a stand on certain values or disvalues. It needs little reflection, however, to see that we don't carry this policy through, and that there are things which we regard as wrong, indeed as *always* wrong, irrespective of alternative viewpoints.

This is another way of saying that we hold to the notion of moral *truth*, that it is possible to say that this action or attitude is truly good, that truly evil; and that it is the human thing to look for the truth, and to live in its light, and that to renounce this search is to abandon our humanity. This is not to say that moral truth is always easy to know, as indeed we have glimpsed already, and it is not to deny the significance of the subjective and the relative. It is to say, though, that when we come to make our judgments we are not reliant merely on some kind of gut instinct about which no argument can be made, but that there is a moral *knowledge* which informs our decisions, and which is a prerequisite for a right decision.

Situation ethics

An approach to a theory of moral decision-making, which came to the fore during the sixties, was what is known as 'situation ethics', associated especially in the United States with the name of Joseph Fletcher. The name points to its central insight, which was that every situation is unique, and that therefore there are no principles or rules that apply in every situation. All you need is love, said the situationists, and you evaluate each situation on its own terms; and what you come up with will be the morally right thing to do.

In *Situation Ethics*[5] Fletcher set out the main lines of his approach in six propositions:

i) Only one 'thing' is intrinsically good; namely love, nothing else at all.

ii) The ruling norm of Christian decision is love, nothing else.

iii) Love and justice are the same, for justice is love distributed, nothing else.

iv) Love wills the neighbour's good whether we like him or not.

v)   Only the end justifies the means, nothing else.

vi)   Love's decisions are made situationally, not prescriptively.

Critics have acknowledged the importance of the situationists'
emphasis on the primacy of love, but have questioned whether
their account of it is coherent or consistent. J. Gustafson, for
example, wrote: '"Love" like "situation" is a word that runs
through Fletcher's book like a greased pig... Nowhere does
Fletcher indicate in a systemic way his various uses of it. It
refers to everything he wants it to refer to'.[6] Less colourfully,
Richard McCormick observed that the theory offers no
satisfactory way of discovering what 'the loving thing' is: 'At
one time [it] is the sum of the consequences of an act, so that
if, by and large, more harm will result, the proposed activity
would be unloving. At other times... this caring is distinct from
the act and its effects, and seems to be only an inner
psychological state'.[7] It seems that on the situationist view *any*
act could be loving, and there is no act which may never be
done.

    A further defect in situationist theory is that it fails to take
account of elements common to moral situations. Enda
McDonagh puts this point thus: 'The uniqueness of the
personal centres or poles in any moral situation gives the
situation itself a uniqueness which cannot be denied but which
does not exclude it entirely from continuity with similar
situations involving other people or the same people at
different times. It is the denial of this continuity which makes
the otherwise valuable insistence of certain situationists on the
uniqueness of the situation ultimately indefensible because it is
unintelligible.'[8]

    In terms of the analysis of sources of moral evaluation into
motive, act and circumstances it will be noticed that what
situationist theory does is to attend to motive and
circumstances but to omit consideration of the character of the
act. But if it is legitimate to overlook what goes on in the act,

any act can be justified in terms of motive and circumstances, and we should be prepared to consider, as Herbert McCabe somewhere said, that even such a manifestly heinous act as the slow roasting of a child to death might be justified.

In making moral decisions, however, we do in fact avail ourselves of principles other than the love commandment in order to arrive at a right decision. And if you inspect your own repertoire of principles, you will see that it is possible to classify them, and the classification is helpful in allowing us to see what we can expect by way of concrete guidance. It should be mentioned that there are several ways of classifying principles; the one here adopted is fairly straightforward, and suits our purposes well.

Conscience and principle

One type of principle which features as part of the information carried by our consciences is exemplified in the statement that 'human life is to be respected'. This signals the necessity of a general attitude toward life which is reverent, constructive, protective and so on. It gives a shape to our choices vis-à-vis human life which ought to ensure a due regard for the life of our fellows, and for the environment in which that life is lived.

On its face, however, this principle tells us nothing about concrete action; it does not tell us what we are to do or refrain from doing in function of our stance of respect. For guidance on concrete action we need other principles or rules which are more concrete and specific. And so, for example, we have a rule such as that 'we ought to come to the help of someone whose life is in danger', or that 'we ought to contribute to charities that have as their object the improvement of living conditions in, say, a developing country'. We also have rules which specify what may *not* be done, as for example the rule that 'we ought not to murder', or that 'killing is wrong'.

Principles of the first type – those that offer a stance and give a general shape to our activities – are called *formal* principles. The second type, exemplified in the proposition that 'we ought not to murder', is *tautological* or tautologous: murder is wrongful killing, and to say that murder is wrong is no more than to say that wrongful killing is wrong. But this doesn't mean that the rule is useless: it is specific and it is concrete; we know that a murder is a killing, even if there is still to be answered the question whether a particular killing is wrongful or not.

For not all killing is wrongful in the sense of its being immoral – an accidental killing (provided of course that the accident wasn't due to negligence), however tragic it may be, doesn't imply moral fault on the part of the person who caused the killing. Additionally the western ethical tradition in general has supported the notion that it is legitimate to kill in self-defence if no other means is feasible, an insight which then becomes an important part of the doctrine of the just war. None of this is to say that killing isn't an *evil*, only that it isn't always a *moral* evil. More of this anon.

The kind of principle of which 'killing is wrong' is an example is known as *material*, and is recognisable by the fact that the subject of the sentence – what is said to be wrong – is a purely material description of an action or omission or state of affairs. This is distinguished from a proposition such as 'murder is wrong'; murder is not simply a description of an action but also carries an evaluative ingredient; murder, as we saw, is *wrongful* killing.

It may be useful to offer examples from two other areas, in order to show that this classification of principle has a general application. Take the area of justice; and analogous to the principle that 'we ought to respect human life' is that which says that 'we ought to do justice' or that 'justice must be done'. Here again we have an injunction to a general stance and attitude, the stance or attitude which prescribes that we ought to give people what is their due, their rights, what is owed to them.

But again the precept tells us nothing concrete, and again in practice we call in aid some more specific principles, positive and negative, for the guidance of our actions. Among the relevant negative principles is one which says that 'stealing is wrong', and another which says that 'taking someone else's property without his or her consent is wrong'. Again we encounter a tautology, for stealing in ethical discourse means wrongful taking, leaving the question whether a particular taking is wrongful or not. Of course, we know that not all taking of someone else's property without consent is wrongful, as when I borrow a friend's pen, having none to hand, and intending to return it as soon as I've finished. Notice again, 'taking someone's property without his or her consent' is a purely *material* description, it indicates only the *matter* of the act, and there is no evaluative note built in.

A third and final set of examples comes from the area of truthfulness, starting with the proposition that 'we ought to be truthful' (or to do the truth, or to respect truth, or something similar). The similarities between this and the other formal principles are obvious: again, a stance and shape are prescribed, but nothing yet is said about what we should do or refrain from doing. What we should refrain from doing, inter alia, is telling lies, and so we have a rule that 'lying is wrong'; and we work also with the notion that 'stating a falsehood, saying what is not the case, is wrong'. But in ethical discourse, lying is wrongful falsehood, and not all falsehood is wrongful; and so again we have a tautology and a purely material description, each with its own characteristics.

A two-fold caveat is in order at this point. First, the foregoing analysis is mainly concerned with *acts*, and the impression might be taken that being moral consists in performing a series of good acts. This may have been to some extent already countered by reference to the importance of motivation and other internal states; it will certainly be balanced when we come to the chapter on 'becoming moral', for there we shall meet the concept of virtue. A second caveat has to do with the fact that our concern has been mainly with prohibitions, with 'thou shalt nots' rather than 'thou shalts'. But we need to be careful not to take or give the impression that morality is negative, primarily a matter of avoiding things. It is important to be able to mark off the bottom line, as the jargon has it, the line below which a value is totally frustrated. But this should not be at the expense of recognising that morality is in the first place positive and constructive, a matter of being and doing; there is a great deal more to respect for life, for example, than refraining from killing people.

Notes

1 Dublin, 1994. Non-inclusive language is in the original English text and because the text is official is retained here and elsewhere in this book.

2 *Quodlib.*3, 27.

3 Aquinas was quite clear that to act *against* conscience is always wrong, even when, as it happens, one's judgment is mistaken, provided the mistake is bona fide. He refrained from saying without qualification that one must always act *according to* conscience, for he found it difficult to think that one might bona fide be mistaken about or ignorant of the moral law. But the logic of his position was that one ought always to follow one's conscience, as the authors of the period of the manuals of moral theology (seventeenth to twentieth centuries) saw. They too, naturally, insisted on the need for due care in the process of informing one's conscience. See Eric D'Arcy, *Conscience and Its Right to Freedom,* London, 1961.

4 As intimated in the Introduction there are various forms of these theories, treated in the various introductions to moral philosophy found in the bibliography. Speaking very roughly one might say that **relativism** holds that moralities are relative to cultures and societies, to time and to place, so that there is no universal or truly objective morality or moral truth; and that **subjectivism**, which may reach similar conclusions, locates moral evaluation in the personal, 'subjective', intuitions or perceptions of each individual.

One of the best short pieces on relativism and associated topics is the characteristically lucid 'Moral Relativism' by Philippa Foot in her *Moral Dilemmas*, Oxford, 2002.

5   London, 1966.

6   *The Christian Century* 83 (1966), 654.

7   *Theological Studies* 27 (1966), 614. A view which sees the rightness or wrongness of an act in terms *solely* of its consequences is a version of **Consequentialism.** In the English-speaking world the best-known exponents of a consequentialist view are probably Jeremy Bentham (1748-1832) and John Stuart Mill (1806-1873), both of whom defended a **Utilitarian** theory of morals. This theory holds that an act is good or right if it conforms to the principle of utility; and utility is explained by Bentham as 'that property in any object, whereby it tends to produce benefit, advantage, pleasure, good, or happiness... or... to prevent the happening of mischief, pain, evil, or unhappiness', *Introduction to the Principles of Morals and Legislation* (1789). Utilitarianism prescribes that in our choices we must seek the greatest good of the greatest number. Bentham held that pleasure was the greatest good (so that what is right is what maximises pleasure), which means that his view is a species of **Hedonism** (from *hedone,* the Greek word for pleasure), a general approach which among its proponents included the Greek philosopher Epicurus (342-270 BCE). Mill's utilitarianism is also said to be hedonistic but an important difference between him and Bentham is that he distinguished between higher and lower qualities of pleasures. An account of these theories may be found in any standard moral philosophy textbook (cf. bibliography), and there is a good account in Walter Sinnott-Armstrong, 'Consequentialism', *The Stanford Encyclopedia of Philosophy (Summer 2003 Edition)*, Edward N. Zalta (ed.), URL <http://plato.stanford.edu/archives/sum2003/entries/consequentialism/>.

The main rival to consequentialist theories is **Deontologism** (Greek *deon* = duty) associated especially with the name of Immanuel Kant (1724-1804). This holds that acts are good or bad *in themselves*, regardless of their consequences, and that what is right is what corresponds to a duty or precept. Deontological theories too are treated in standard textbooks; and see Robert Johnson, 'Kant's Moral Philosophy', *The Stanford Encyclopedia of Philosophy (Spring 2004 Edition)*, Edward N. Zalta (ed.), URL

<http://plato.stanford.edu/archives/spr2004/entries/kant-moral/>. It could be said that the approach taken by Catholic moral theology generally is a modified deontologism, i.e that there are *some* acts which are good or bad in themselves: see later in this chapter and chapter four.

8   *Gift and Call*, Dublin, 1975, 31.

4

Moral Dilemmas

The mainline Christian moral theological tradition was familiar with the question of dilemmas, and has developed some approaches which are helpful. Soon we shall look at some examples of dilemmas, but for now we may think of them generally as situations of inescapable evil: whatever we choose to do, some evil will be involved. An obvious response is that we should choose the lesser of two evils, and this makes sense. If an evil is what is contrary to flourishing, it only makes sense, in a situation of inescapable evil, to do as little evil as possible. But the apparent simplicity of this is deceptive, for one of the evils involved may be a *moral* evil; and moral evil may never be done no matter what good is to be achieved. Again, this makes sense: if what is evil is opposed to human flourishing, it would be wrong to choose to do it freely and deliberately. The full meaning of this should emerge shortly.

Universal norms?
A preliminary question, however, is that of the universality or universalisability of moral principles or norms, the question whether there are some norms or principles which always hold, and which may never be breached, no matter what the consequences. These are sometimes called 'absolutes' or

absolute moral principles, by which is meant principles which are exceptionless and unchanging, which hold always and everywhere, and which we cannot envisage being revised.

The question arises about them in the present context because if there are such principles they will trump other types, so that in a dilemma they prevail absolutely. In Catholic teaching one may not for example directly take innocent life, and in a dilemma from which this appears to be the only escape it may not be resorted to. A short answer to our question is that formal and tautologous principles – those of the first and second types in our analysis – are universal, unchanging, immutable, exceptionless; but that those of the third type are not.

It is obvious that the first and second types are universal and exceptionless: it would make no sense to say that we need not respect human life, or that injustice may now be done in aid of some other good, or that it is no longer necessary to have regard for the truth. In addition, it is, of course, self-contradictory to say that murder may sometimes be justified, for this means that wrongful killing is sometimes right; as it would be self-contradictory to say that wrongful taking, or wrongful falsehood, is sometimes right. Hence once a principle is identified as formal or tautologous, it *must* be said of it that it is universal, unchanging, exceptionless, absolute, and so on.

Not so in the case of a purely material proposition, and the reason for this is simple: an act to be evaluated morally must be taken *together with* circumstances and intention, and in the absence of reference to these we are unable to say whether it was morally right or wrong. Let us say we hear that a neighbour has been killed; we do not instantly conclude to murder – or indeed to anything, until we've learned what the circumstances are, and whether the killing was deliberate and not accidental or, if an accident, whether due to wilful negligence. Notice that it is usually possible to say that a particular act is *nearly* always wrong, and so it is quite in order to teach 'thou shalt not kill', or that one shouldn't take another's property without the owner's consent, or that one shouldn't utter falsehoods. You could say that 'as a rule', killing (or whatever) is wrong, and indeed (as with killing) exceptions must be considered rare. There is no need to interrogate ourselves every day as to how much killing or taking of another's property or telling falsehoods is likely to be justified in our case today.

The question of exception can arise, however, and it arises if there is a clash of values in a given situation, and so a clash of principles of the third kind, the rules which aim to protect the values. For then we must decide which of the two rules we should follow, and to keep one must mean to break the other. Suppose for example you are asked for a reference for someone, including the question whether that person has ever had problems with drug taking; and suppose that in confidence you know from the person himself or herself that drug taking was at one time indeed a problem. Normally in a reference one is expected to 'say what is the case', and falsehood or evasion is wrong; and normally also one is expected to keep a confidence. But to say what is the case here will be to betray a confidence, and to keep the confidence will involve deception. What is one to do?

Act of double effect
Associated especially (though not exclusively) with Catholic moral theology there has evolved an approach to the resolution of moral dilemmas known as the doctrine or principle of the *act of double effect*. The significance of the name is that in a dilemma our choice of act will have at least two effects, one good and one bad. If I choose to reveal the drug problem I shall have preserved the value of material truthfulness but broken a trust, whereas if I choose to keep the confidence it will be at the expense of the value of truthfulness. But we saw that in any dilemma I must first be sure that the alternatives don't involve

what is *morally* evil, for one may never do a moral evil no matter what the good anticipated. The doctrine of the act of double effect is meant to assist in ensuring attention to all relevant factors.

What the doctrine says may be summarised as follows: where a choice will have both good and evil results or aspects one must have regard to four conditions.

1 The act must not be immoral in itself.
2 The evil effect must not be *directly* intended.
3 The good effect must not come *through* or *by means of* the evil.
4 There must be a proportionate reason for allowing the evil to happen.

The first condition is sometimes put by saying that the act must be good or at least neutral; it follows from the proposition that it doesn't make sense to opt for what is morally wrong. The second reflects the fact that one may speak of permitting an effect which one doesn't in fact want or intend, as when a pregnant woman undergoes treatment or an operation for womb cancer which has the incidental effect of causing the death of the foetus. The third condition amplifies the notion that one may never do a moral evil so that good might come of it. Finally, the fourth introduces an idea long familiar in the tradition, which is that there must be a due proportion between the good and evil in a given choice – one may not occasion a major evil for the sake of a minor good.

Two examples may help to illustrate the way the doctrine works.[1] The first is the case already alluded to, now fortunately rare, in which a pregnant woman is discovered to have cancer of the womb. If she has a hysterectomy or undergoes chemotherapy or radiotherapy the cancer will be cured but the foetus will die. Applying the doctrine of double effect one can see that the choice of an operation or of treatment accords with the first condition, for neither is 'immoral in itself', each is what is normally and uncontroversially done where a woman has womb cancer. Nor is the death of the foetus *directly* intended: it is a by-product of the procedure intended to cure the cancer, and is not wanted either for itself or as a means to an end. For it is not through the death of the foetus that the mother is saved, and the medical team would take every possible step to ensure that it need not come about. The notion of proportionate reason – the fourth condition – is technical, and we must see in a moment what it means, but for now we can think of it as a reason which is sufficiently grave.

Compare this case to one in which an unmarried girl who lives with her parents becomes pregnant by a married man. Her mother has a serious heart condition, and there is every reason to fear that discovery of the daughter's situation will lead to her death. The daughter cannot plausibly leave home, so having the baby and having it adopted is a course of action which will not provide a solution. What about the doctrine of double effect?

Someone who considers that whether to have an abortion or not is a matter solely for the choice of the woman will not, strictly speaking, have a dilemma at this point (which is not to say that she won't have a painful decision); but for anyone who subscribes to the view that to take the life of the foetus in this instance is a directly intended option for death, a decision for abortion fails on at least three grounds. First, it cannot be said that a termination of pregnancy in this case is good or neutral: it is the directly willed bringing about of a death, and so violates the second condition. Thirdly, it is through the death that the good – the continued life of the grandmother – is achieved. We need not consider whether there was proportionate reason, for the doctrine applies only when *all four conditions* are met.

The judicial murder and the runaway tram
Another well-known pair of cases are those known respectively as the judicial murder and the runaway tram case.

In the first, based on a true story in a southern US state in the early part of the last century, a white woman was killed by a black man, and a riot among the white population – occasioned in part also by the fact that law enforcement in the town was poor – resulted in five black people being taken hostage. The authorities in the person of the sheriff were warned that unless the culprit was found the hostages would be killed. The culprit had in fact fled the jurisdiction, and there was no possibility of capturing him. An elderly black man, however, had recently been arrested for vagrancy, and the sheriff thought that by causing him to be convicted of the white woman's murder, the lives of the hostages would be saved. Conviction carried the death penalty.

That this course of action cannot be justified under the double effect doctrine is evident if we consider that what the sheriff proposes is the directly intended killing of an innocent man. This means that it fails to meet either the first condition, or the second; and neither does it conform to the third, since it is through the death of the vagrant that the good result, the sparing of the hostages' lives, would take place. Again, we need not for the moment consider proportionality – failing to meet the first three conditions is more than enough to disqualify the option of causing the old man's death.

In the case of the runaway tram a driver was bringing a tram from one depot to another and saw that there were five men working on the line ahead. He immediately tried to stop the tram but the brakes failed, and the tram went hurtling toward the five men. The only alternative was to divert the tram to a spur line, on which, however, one man was working. Anyone would have the utmost sympathy for someone in the driver's position, and one can recognise also that the stress of the moment must affect whatever decision he made. But our question just now is not about the personal morality of the driver, it is about whether deflecting to the spur, occasioning the death of one man, in preference to continuing on the main line, thus killing five, meets the conditions of the doctrine of the act of double effect.

The first question to be addressed again is how the action is to be described, and the action in question is correctly described as 'deflecting to a spur'. The driver does not wish to kill the man working on the spur, he doesn't need the death for his purposes, and one may suppose that he would do anything in his power to ensure that the man is saved. He is moreover performing an act which would be the normal one in such a case if it weren't for the presence of the one man, and it cannot be said of it that it is immoral in itself. The driver is in a situation of unavoidable evil – death will ensue whichever choice he makes – and he is trying to minimise the evil. So the choice of deflection to the spur accords with the condition that the act be indifferent or good, as well as with the second and third conditions, since he doesn't will the death of the man, nor is it by means of the man's death that the five lives are spared. But what of the fourth condition, that there must be a proportionate reason for allowing the evil to happen? Earlier we adopted the simple explanation that the reason must be sufficiently weighty; but this is vague, and now it is time to clarify the sense of this condition.

Proportionate reason
The notion of proportionality goes back at least to the writings of St Thomas, and was especially familiar to students of medical ethics in the Catholic tradition. An older account said that a reason for doing something which may have normally unacceptable aspects is proportionate when the good to be derived from a choice of action was commensurate with or outweighed the bad. But this leaves the sometimes difficult – some would say insoluble – question, how do you decide that the good outweighs the bad? In the course of a debate about the scope of the applicability of the idea, a useful clarification was offered by Richard McCormick.

McCormick said that reason is proportionate when (a) a value at least equal to the value sacrificed is at stake; (b) there is no other way of protecting the value here and now; and (c) the manner of protecting the value here and now is not such as will undermine it. Put another way, it might be said that reason is not proportionate when the value sacrificed is greater, when there are alternative solutions, or when the action involved in protecting a value are of a kind which in fact undermines the value.

Applied to the judicial murder case, the principle of proportionality requires attention to the question whether there is a parity or otherwise of value involved in the choice to have the old man executed in order to save the five – to which it might be said that in each case what is at stake is the value of life.[2] It would of course also be imperative that every other way of solving the problem is tried, but even if there is parity of value and no other way, a decision to frame the old man would fail on the third test. For what would be involved would be the directly intended killing of an innocent man, a course of action which of its nature must undermine the value of life.

By contrast, consider the tram driver's case. Again, we can grant parity of value and also that there is no other way to avoid killing the five men. What of the third test? Is a decision to deflect to the spur the kind of decision that must undermine the value of life? What does the driver choose? He chooses to deflect to a spur, an action which is not of itself a wrong action. He foresees the death of the man working on the spur, but he doesn't will this or want it. If the five are to be saved it is not because one man has died, it is not through, or by means of, the death that the lives of the five are spared. This is in contrast to the sheriff, who needs and must will the death of the vagrant if his purposes are to be fulfilled.

Comparable considerations apply in the two abortion cases. The pregnant woman and her medical team will not want the death of the foetus and will take every step to avoid it. They do not need it for their purpose, for it is not through the death of the foetus that the mother's life is saved but through successful surgery or therapy. Not so in the case of the girl whose mother is ill: the death of the foetus is a prerequisite of saving the mother's life, and so she must will it and intend it in the most direct way. In the first case, therefore, the manner of protecting the value, i.e. of saving the mother, is not inherently inimical to the value of life; in the second, a direct assault upon innocent life, it manifestly is.

A final application may help show how the doctrine of double effect can illuminate a moral dilemma. During the first Gulf war a UN special operations unit was camped outside Baghdad, with the two-fold mission of gathering intelligence and of helping guide smart missiles to their destination. The mission was regarded as crucial to the achievement of an early victory, and the unit was charged with keeping its operations secret at all costs. But a fourteen-year-old shepherd girl strayed into the camp, and so the unit's leaders were presented with a dilemma. If she were let go, their whereabouts would be known and the mission, as it seemed, fatally compromised. But under the Geneva Conventions they were forbidden to take her captive, even for a short time. Could they have availed themselves of the doctrine of double effect so as to justify killing her?

The act would have had to be described as the directly willed killing of an innocent person, and so would have met none of the conditions. This is clear as regards the first two, and clear also as regards the third, for it is through the death of the girl that the camp's purposes would have been safeguarded. But it is clear enough also for the fourth condition, since the manner of preserving the values to be preserved would have involved a direct subversion of a core insight – that it is never right directly to procure the death of an innocent person; and so the condition of proportionality must have been breached also.[3]

The distinction between what is directly and indirectly willed, and indeed the whole of the doctrine of double effect, plays a part in the formulation of what has become known as the doctrine of the just war. It is a condition of that doctrine that non-combatants must not *directly* be killed. But the justification for indirect killing of civilians – collateral damage, as this is sometimes euphemistically called – is often glib; and in particular it is forgotten that *all four conditions* of the double effect doctrine must be verified, so that the evil in what looks like an indirectly willed fatality is aggravated by its being a disproportionate price to pay for the good intended in the strike which caused the death.

Hairsplitting?

Some readers may feel impatient with the sort of analysis involved in the application of the double effect doctrine or the principle of proportionate reason. They may feel that such analysis reduces human dilemmas to the level of a conundrum in some abstract order of logic unrelated to real life. Or they may think that it involves hairsplitting of a kind which is especially objectionable considering that the dilemmas usually in question when these ideas are invoked are matters, literally, of life and death. Comparable reactions have been found among the ranks of professional ethicians (including some moral theologians), especially in reference to the distinction between what is directly willed or intended and what is merely permitted.[4]

It would be foolish indeed to try to offer a quick solution to a debate which is unquestionably complex, but perhaps one may venture some remarks in support of the approach embodied in the double effect doctrine in general, and in the direct/indirect distinction in particular. First, it can hardly be wrong to try to find a structured way toward resolving moral dilemmas, rather than wander about in a 'situationist' fog. And while there are aspects and applications of the direct/indirect

distinction which are not uncontroversial, does the distinction
nevertheless not answer to a plausible intuition? What *is* our
basic intuition concerning the difference between the killing
involved in, say, the judicial murder case and that of the
runaway tram? Do we really think that what the sheriff did *was
morally equivalent to* what the driver did? And if we don't, how is
the difference to be expressed? Do we not *need* some such
distinction?[5]

The philosopher Anthony Kenny has suggested that what
gave the doctrine of double effect a bad name was its
association with the theory of direction of intention satirised
by Pascal in *Lettres Provinciales*[6]. I think we should have to grant
that the mental gymnastics of some of the moral theologians
known as casuists lent themselves easily to satire, but the
casuistry in question was a debased one and very different from
the humane and sophisticated efforts of better authors in their
search to reconcile moral principle with the complex and
difficult demands of life. The persistence of the double effect
doctrine suggests a sturdiness and a continuing usefulness, even
if its use has not been trouble-free. It is not, I think, fanciful to
imagine that further discussion will lead to further refinement
of the concepts and devices which it employs. But one would
be very surprised indeed were it to be abandoned.

Another caveat
As the last chapter did on negative norms, this has concentrated
on moral dilemmas, and for a similar reason: both themes give
rise to important theoretical as well as practical questions. But
of course the moral life is not – mercifully – a series of
dilemmas. Again, attention to the positive aspects of morality,
and especially now to the significance of the concept of virtue,
will help keep the picture balanced.

Notes

1   These examples are commonplace in texts on moral theology and
     moral philosophy: see for example, V. MacNamara, *The Truth in
     Love*, Dublin, 1988.

2   There are of course also the values of justice and truthfulness, each
     of which is sacrificed in a process involving false accusation and
     conviction of an innocent; but it is enough for our purposes to
     consider the life values only.

3   The unit in fact decided to let the girl go, and they immediately
     struck camp and moved to another place.

4   There is a particular problem with this distinction in legal systems
     such as the Irish (and English and those of most of the United
     States). In these systems one is held responsible for the 'reasonably
     foreseeable' consequences of one's acts, and of course on that view
     the fact that something was 'merely permitted' (i.e. only indirectly
     intended) could not justify or excuse. It is therefore of great
     significance that in England, in cases such as that of the conjoined
     twins Jodie and Mary, judges have found themselves as it were
     reaching for some such distinction as the direct/indirect, and that
     academic legal discussion displays more sympathy for it than was
     formerly usual.

5   On the need for a distinction, though she disagrees with the
     doctrine, see Philippa Foot, 'The Problem of Abortion and the
     Doctrine of the Double Effect' in *Virtues and Vices*, Oxford, 1978,
     19ff.

6   A. Kenny, *The Anatomy of the Soul*, Oxford, 1973, Appendix: 'The
     History of Intention in Ethics', 140. Incidentally Jeremy Bentham
     spoke of direct and 'oblique' intention, of which Kenny has written
     that '[t]he distinction between direct and oblique intention
     corresponds to the scholastic one between intention and foresight'.
     Kenny, op. cit., 142

5

Becoming Moral

If morality is the art of right relationship with our neighbour and with the world around us, how do we become proficient in this art? We have seen that a critical part of the necessary equipment is conscience, and so a critical aspect of becoming morally proficient is the acquisition of a mature conscience. But being moral is not just a matter of *knowing* right from wrong, it is also a matter of *doing*. And proficiency in doing what is right and good is achieved through the practice of virtue. In this chapter we shall see something of the way in which conscience develops, and something of what is involved in the cultivation of the virtues.

Are we born with a conscience? Some ways of talking about conscience suggest that we are, as when it is sometimes said that it is an *innate* capacity, or when a religious person says that conscience is implanted in us by God. But to say that we are born with a conscience is to imply that a newly born child can distinguish between right and wrong, and of course this is manifestly not the case. It is better to say that we are born with a capacity for conscience, with the makings of a conscience, and that our conscience is made or achieved through the normal processes of human education.

Education here is to be understood in the broadest sense, and not just as formal education. It is arguable that conscience is being made even while a child is in the womb, for even at that stage it is picking up signals as to what life is like; and certainly once it is born, in its interactions with the mother and with whomever else may be involved in its nurture, it is constantly being given an impression of what it is to be a human being in the world.

The super-ego

A more systematic process of creating or forming a conscience comes when a parent or parent figure begins to impart elementary dos and don'ts, signifying approval when the child complies, disapproval when it doesn't. One way of understanding this process is in terms of an account offered by Freud.[1] For him, a child is first a bundle of needs and wants which cry out – literally indeed – to be satisfied; this aspect of our make-up he termed the *id*. But it requires also to be domesticated or socialised, 'trained' to become an autonomous member of the human community. This process begins when a parent or parent figure starts directing and correcting its behaviour; and as it gradually internalises the commands and prohibitions thus taught it is acquiring a *super-ego* or infantile conscience.

The most basic need is the need for love, and, for the infant, love is signalled through the approval, normally first, of the mother. When the child conforms it is rewarded with a smile or a cuddle or other sign of the mother's pleasure; when it disobeys, a frown betokens disapproval. Since the most basic need of the child is the need for love, it learns to subject its other needs to this, and will behave in such a way as to ensure approval and avoid rejection. As every parent knows, it won't behave rightly unfailingly, and in particular it is likely to 'test' any other minders it may have, attempting to discover whether that person's rules are the same as those of the parents.

This draws attention to an important aspect of this early process of regulating a child's behaviour, which is that the rules are so associated with the rule-giver that a change of rule-giver

'suggests' a change of rules. Another way of putting this is to
say that the rules are *external*, they come from outside, and
continue to be linked with a figure outside of the child, and are
not yet internalised or appropriated or made the child's own. Of
course they are in time internalised to the point where they
remain in the memory or in the imagination, so that the child
can recall what happened when last it kicked the cat, or
imagine what will happen if the mother finds it raiding the
fridge. But they are still the parent's or minder's rules, not yet
adopted as the settled convictions of the young person.

This can only come about when the child learns to see the
point of the rules which have been given; and this is where a
more formal education process plays a part. No mother,
attempting to ensure that a three-year-old won't burn herself in
the fire, will give a lecture on the properties of fire and on what
happens when fire is brought in contact with the skin. But
when in due course a child begins to be able to reason, it's
appropriate that injunctions to good conduct are accompanied
by an explanation as to why this, rather than some other form
of behaviour, is to be preferred.

One might characterise the 'conscience' of the young child,
therefore, as having three features. First, the rules come from
outside, from a parent or other authority figure, and continue
to be identified with that figure. Second, the rules will be
simple, black and white; for the child is unable to take in
nuance, and the main thing will be to get it to behave in such a
way that it will do no harm to itself or anyone or anything else.
Third, the child conforms for fear of disapproval, for fear of
losing love; it behaves, in other words, out of its need for
continued love.

An adult conscience
An adult or mature conscience, by contrast, has the following
characteristics. First, the rules have been internalised, in a
process in which the young person comes to see the point of

this or that injunction, and adopts it as part of his or her own repertoire of value and principle. (The process may of course involve the jettisoning of some rules, for not all of what is passed on by a generation will recommend itself to the next.) Second, the picture one has of right and wrong is no longer black and white. The repertoire will contain some 'absolutes', values and principles which are the bedrock of the person's morality; but there will be an awareness also of the existence of grey areas, and an ability to cope with the grey. Third, the person will act, not out of a need to be loved and approved, or out of a fear of losing approval, but out of a will to love, a conscious option for what is positive and creative in one's dealings with others.

If this is what moral maturity is, one might ask whether there are many who are morally mature. Perhaps one should say that at our best our behaviour exhibits the characteristics just noted, but that we are not always at our best. Sometimes we operate more or less unreflectingly with notions of right and wrong inherited from 'tradition' or from our peers, notions that we haven't really made our own. Sometimes also, fearful of ambiguity and of life's grey areas, we opt for black-and-white solutions, or look to an authority which will tell us in plain terms what we are to do. And sometimes we act (or not) out of a fear of loss of 'love', not wanting to lose the approval of authority or the neighbours or other peers.

Eric Fromm has written of 'fear of freedom',[2] observing that, to adapt Eliot, humankind cannot bear very much autonomy. His point is that freedom, much as we cherish it, is conducive to anxiety, and that after a time of anxiety we may seek relief in simple solutions. He takes the examples of Germany and Italy in the twenties – periods of permissiveness and of personal freedom which brought their own anxieties, and times in which it was therefore easy for the authoritarianisms of nazism and fascism to take root. This is a plausible analysis, and one might wonder whether something comparable could be said of the decades which have followed the sixties.

The education of conscience

The movement from the infantile or super-ego dominated 'conscience' to moral maturity is importantly dependent on a moral education which not only proposes values and rules for behaviour but which also offers the reasons why these values and rules ought to be adopted, and which encourages a critical appropriation of them.[3] It's worth recalling, again, though, that moral reasoning isn't 'ratiocination', that there is indeed a cognitive dimension but that this does not exclude the affective and the imaginative, so that a worthwhile moral education must include also education of the emotions and in the use of the imagination.[4]

So it is that there is a role for story and symbol as well as for argument, and that what goes on in a literature or art class may be as important for moral education as what transpires in formal religious or moral education. Not that art or literature is to be used in a crudely moralistic fashion, rather that a poem or picture or novel be allowed to speak for itself, offering its insight into the human condition, engaging our imagination, engendering our empathy, perhaps refining our perception and our feelings in the way that great art can.

A simple example may illustrate what I have in mind here. Frank O'Connor's *Guests of the Nation* tells what happens when two Englishmen are taken captive by the IRA during the War of Independence. The men and their captors play cards together and chat, and gradually make friends, in spite of the fact that they are at war. And when the order comes for the prisoners' execution the captors are saddened, and don't want to carry out the order. But carry it out they must, and the bleakness of their feelings is conveyed in the last lines of the story.

What is revealed in this story is a common humanity underlying the roles which the protagonists are required to play, and undercutting the hostility toward each other that the conflict reflects and engenders. And the sadness and futility of war is conveyed, as a naturally begotten friendship gives way to the rules and conventions of warfare. We are not given a lecture on 'humanity' or the brotherhood and sisterhood of peoples, nor on the evils of warfare. But our imaginations and our feelings are engaged, and we are drawn into the story in such a way that we feel with the characters, and can empathise with the narrator as he looks at the sky; 'and the birds and the bloody stars were all far away, and I was somehow very small and very lonely. And anything that ever happened to me after I never felt the same about again'.

Education in virtue

The education of conscience is only one aspect of the process of moral education for, as remarked earlier, it is one thing to *know* but another to *do*, and morality is an art which is to be practised. One way of looking at this is to recall that freedom as well as reason is at the heart of our capacity to be moral, and that freedom no less than reason needs education. Education in and of and for freedom is a complex task, and there is a role for 'training' in this or that piece of good behaviour, as when the young person is asked to help with the housework or to do the shopping for an ailing neighbour. Such training will not necessarily ensure fixed attitudes of helpfulness or of concern, but they may help, and without them it is difficult to see what the prospects are.

A difficulty also lies in the fact that there must come a time at which a parent or teacher 'lets go', so that the young person may *practise* the exercise of freedom, even at the cost of making mistakes. It is much easier to say this than to do it, for no parent will want their son or daughter to come to harm or to cause harm, and the temptation of the conscientious parent may be to be vigilant beyond what is healthy. But excessive or protracted vigilance is likely to provoke resentment, as an adolescent is trying to find adult feet; and it will very likely also breed hypocrisy, for the temptation will be to appear to conform whilst behaving otherwise when out of sight.

This may be an appropriate place at which to draw attention to an important modern emphasis in the literature of moral theology and philosophy, the emergence (or re-emergence) of what is known as virtue ethics.[5] In the preceding chapter we discussed the workings of conscience in terms of its function of judging, antecedently or consequently, the rightness or wrongness of particular acts, and we gave particular attention to the question of resolving moral dilemmas. All of this was necessary, but it has the potential to mislead inasmuch as it focuses attention on individual acts, for it might thereby give the impression that the moral life consists in a series of discrete acts. This would be at the expense of the insight that our acts exhibit *patterns*, and that the pattern of one's actions is a critical ingredient in moral appraisal and moral growth.

Underlying this is the idea that what we *do* reflects and expresses what we *are*. If I am disposed to give people their due, I am likely to pay my bills. Another way of putting this is to say that if I have the virtue of justice, I will habitually give people their due (and so, *inter alia*, pay my bills). Similarly with, say, truthfulness: to have a habit of truthfulness will mean that I am likely to speak the truth on any particular occasion. One might think of a virtue as a settled disposition to behave in a certain – morally praiseworthy – way, as when justice is defined as a perpetual and settled will to give each his or her due.

One of the reasons for the re-emergence of the concept of virtue in ethical discourse is a growing scepticism as to the usefulness of moral rules. This arises from a recognition of the factual pluralism in moral value and principles as between societies and indeed now within them. What is made of this is that moral rules are *relative* to cultures, to societies, to communities and to situations, so that there aren't universal, or even usefully general, norms. From this it is concluded that the best that can be hoped for is the inculcation within communities of good *practices*, which preserve the community's values and translate them into daily living.

It was already suggested in chapter four that the relativity of moral value and principle can be overstated, and that there are some principles which can correctly be termed universal. People differ as to whether euthanasia for example is morally licit or not, but no serious person will question the need to treat the dying with loving care. The dignity of each human being is acknowledged throughout the world now, even if particular societies engage in practices which do not respect that dignity; and equality is proclaimed even in places where it is manifestly not honoured.

But there is another reason why one should avoid too sharp a disjunction between virtue ethics and an ethic that is act-centred. This is expressed by William Frankena as follows: 'It is hard to see how a morality of principles can get off the ground except through the development of dispositions to act in accordance with principles... on the other hand, one cannot conceive of traits of character except as including dispositions and tendencies to act in certain ways in certain circumstances'[6]. One will not be inclined to act virtuously unless disposed to do so, and unless in the habit of so doing; but how could one be said to be 'disposed' or 'in the habit' unless one were found to act in a particular way.

Moral failure

This has an application to the question of moral failure as well as to growth in virtue, in the way it directs attention to the *pattern* of our activities. For if what counts is the pattern, then individual lapses need not betoken major failure; the just man falls seven times a day, and the wrong-doer may always repent. In recent Catholic moral theology this way of looking at moral failure has come to be associated with what has been called the 'fundamental option'. The idea here is that, as already said, the choices that we make both express what we are and shape our future choices, so that behind or underneath the history of our individual choices is revealed a basic stance vis-à-vis the good, our 'fundamental option'.

This is consistent with modern psychology's insight concerning the historicity of our lives, the fact that we are always in process of becoming. It coheres also with what has been called the law of gradualness, which embodies the truth that we become good – just, truthful, compassionate, loving – only gradually; and it sits well with the classical distinction between objective and subjective morality. But of course it should not lead to self-delusion or an easy extenuation of fault, as when we make light of individual actions or trivialise them. Our actions remain expressive of who we are, and to fail even once in justice is to reflect some lack of that virtue in us. Additionally our choices shape what we shall be in the future, and to have chosen unjustly is to have set ourselves upon a path in which injustice may be chosen again.[7]

Notes

1   An account of this, with interesting applications, is found in John W. Glaser, 'Conscience and the Superego: a Key Distinction', in C. Ellis Nelson (ed.), *Conscience: Theological and Psychological Perspectives*, New York, 1973, 167ff. A summary is in Richard Gula, *Reason Informed by Faith*, New York/Mahwah, 1989, 127.

2   Eric Fromm, *The Fear of Freedom*, London, 1942, 1960.

3   The process of moral development has been studied by, among others, Lawrence Kohlberg; see for example his *Collected Papers on Moral Development and Moral Education*, Harvard, 1973, and *The Philosophy of Moral Development*, San Francisco, 1981. Some of Kohlberg's findings have been criticised by Carol Gilligan in *In A Different Voice: Psychological Theory and Women's Development*, Harvard, 1982, on the basis that his work does not take account of what she argues is a different experience of morality and moral development among girls and women. Contributions to the ensuing debate, together with bibliography, are reproduced in

Mary Jeanne Larrabee (ed.), *An Ethic of Care: Feminist and Interdisciplinary Perspectives*, New York/London, 1993. A good introduction to Kohlberg's work is Ronald Duska and Mariellen Whelan, *Moral Development: a Guide to Piaget and Kohlberg*, New York, 1975. A very different approach, of special interest in the context of 'virtue ethics' (see below), is in Craig Dykstra, *Vision and Character: an Educator's Alternative to Kohlberg*, New York/Ramsey 1981. A very useful general treatment is 'Moral Character: Becoming a Good Person', in William Cosgrave, *Christian Living Today: Essays in Moral and Pastoral Theology*, Dublin, 2001, 23 ff. See also Cosgrave, 'Our Emotional Life and Moral Living', op. cit., 41.

4   See for example Philip S. Keane, *Christian Ethics and the Imagination*, Ramsey, 1984; Mark Johnson, *Moral Imagination*, Chicago/London, 1993. (Both give further references.)

5   Two books which will help further study of this topic are Jean Porter, *The Recovery of Virtue*, Louisville, 1990, and Roger Crisp and Michael Slote (eds), *Virtue Ethics*, Oxford, 1997. The latter, a volume in the 'Oxford Readings in Philosophy' series, is a collection of some of the most authoritative writing on virtue ethics.

6   *Ethics*, 2nd edn, Englewood Cliffs 1973, 65.

7   On sin generally see Hugh Connolly, *Sin*, New York, 2002 and Sean Fagan, *Has Sin Changed?*, Dublin, 1978.

6

Morality and Religion

Up to now we have been examining morality as it were 'in itself'; that is, as an aspect of human experience found in all times and places, and not confined to people who are religious or Christian. Now it is time to ask what difference Christian faith makes, and it will be useful if we look first at religion and morality in general terms. For there are questions and problems of a general kind when it comes to envisaging relationships between morality and religion. And we might start with the question (granted especially that there are people who are not religious but who are certainly moral): where might religion enter the picture when one is trying to understand the moral life?

A preliminary task is that of settling upon a working definition of religion – not an easy task, as the writing of such as Emile Durkheim, William James, Rudolf Otto and Mircea Eliade shows. The term might refer to a belief system and / or a system of practices, or to an institution which embodies and transmits beliefs and practices from one generation to the next. What I have in mind primarily at this point is the first sense, a system of beliefs and practices, and I shall focus for the moment on beliefs. Religions generally provide for certain practices, and Christianity certainly does, but consideration of these will be conveniently postponed until we come to examine the notion of spirituality.

But now another question arises: what are religious beliefs about? One can't immediately answer something like 'a supreme being' or 'a god', for Buddhism is one of the major world religions though it doesn't involve belief in a god.[1] Nor, therefore, can one say that religious practices are aimed at contact with a god or supreme being, for again in Buddhism practices of contemplation and awareness and so on, are not in aid of contact with a god.[2]

Religious moralities

Yet perhaps it is possible to say that religion involves belief in an unseen dimension in life, commonly in a god or supreme being, and religious practice is aimed at putting one in contact with that dimension. Religions commonly involve not only beliefs about God, though; they usually prescribe also a way of life which includes direction on how we relate to each other. Sometimes, as in each of the major religions, albeit in differing ways, the manner in which people relate to each other in this life is seen to have a bearing on a future life.

So religion characteristically entails a morality, in that the religions require adherents to live according to certain values and ideals, and one can hardly imagine a belief system which merited the name of religion which was indifferent to how people relate to each other as well as to the transcendent.[3] The matter can be looked at also from the side of morality, as was seen briefly in our introductory chapter. For the experience of morality gives rise to questions whose answer lies in one's world-view, and many people's world-view is religious. So, for example, one might ask whether there is a significance in right living which is more than meets the eye, whether human flourishing is more than might be guessed at from an examination of the prerequisites for well-being in the world, whether morality has any future apart from what can be

achieved imperfectly in the here and now, whether there is any
'salvation' from the failure in which we so often find ourselves
trapped.

The good atheist

It is possible to answer these questions in a way that is not
religious in any usual sense, and everyone knows a 'good
atheist' or agnostic, someone of high moral standards who
does not believe in God. On the other hand there are people
who cannot for themselves ground morality satisfactorily
without envisaging it in terms of God's will or God's law,
though it might be argued that this is no more than a
psychological necessity in any particular case. Even the
sentiment attributed to Dostoievski, 'If God does not exist,
then everything is permitted',[4] need be no more than the *cri de
coeur* of a particularly religious temperament. And attempts to
construct a 'proof' for the existence of God based upon the
existence of a moral order have not been persuasive.[5]

It can perhaps be argued more strongly that morality must
imply some kind of 'spirituality'. We shall see more of this in
chapter ten, but for the moment a modest point may be made.
This is that most spiritualities make provision for contemplative
or meditative practices which aim at enabling contact with
one's 'deepest self', and the kind of discernment required in
moral judgment, especially in an important or complex matter,
bespeaks a contemplative or meditative mode. As the *Catechism*
puts it, 'it is important for every person to be sufficiently
present to himself in order to hear and follow the voice of his
conscience' (1779)[6]. This is a frame of mind that is achieved
only when one disposes oneself especially, and it is not
normally achievable apart from 'practice'.

A religious person who envisages the moral life in terms of
response to God's call – understood of course metaphorically –
will see such practices as attuning oneself to God's 'voice'. In
Christian theology the voice of conscience is explicitly equated

with the voice of God, as when *Gaudium et Spes* says that conscience is our most secret core and sanctuary, where we are alone with God whose voice echoes in our depths.[7] As we saw in chapter three, this is by no means an invitation to some kind of pietistic or pseudo-mystical attitude which would divinise whim or caprice. *Gaudium et Spes*, following Paul, also speaks of conscience as a 'law' inscribed in our hearts by God.[8] There is a cognitive dimension in moral discernment, one needs to 'think things through'; and in the Christian view discernment takes place in any case within the Christian community, as we shall also later see.

Morality and religion: Judaeo-Christian traditions

It is important not to envisage relationships between religion and morality in such a way as to distort either dimension. This is most obviously done when morality is thought of in crudely legal terms, that is, as a set of laws governing human behaviour analogous to the laws laid down by the human sovereign, God being the lawmaker and also the judge in the case of the moral law.

There may appear to be a warrant for this in the Judaeo-Christian tradition itself, where there is frequent reference to God's law, and to God as author of the Law, as well as to God's judgment, and indeed the reward or punishment which follow our life in the world. Scholars say that the Hebrew Torah, often translated as 'Law', is more properly translated as 'Teachings'; yet that doesn't relieve the impression that the ordinances of the Old Testament are God's *law*, since there are many 'commandments', and in the first place the ten prescriptions of the Decalogue.

But we need not think it odd that God should have been imaged in this way, for humans picture God after their own experience, and their experience of leadership or rulership would have included seeing the ruler as lawmaker and as judge.[9] This was true not just of biblical times but also of early and medieval Christianity; and indeed in the manuals of moral theology – textbooks used in the training of clergy from the seventeenth to the twentieth centuries – the connection made between God and morality evokes the figure of the absolute ruler who possessed supreme legislative, executive and judicial power. Nor was the concept of God as lawgiver confined to Judaeo-Christianity or Islam, as the writings of Plato and other Greek philosophers show.

Morality – a 'divine command'?

Against this background there arose a question, canvassed first by Plato and again by the medieval theologians, whether certain behaviours are good because commanded by God, or whether God commands them because they are good. Thus, Socrates asks Euthyphro whether God commands 'holy' things because they are holy, or whether things are holy because God commands them. Plato's answer is the former, as Aquinas and his followers later attested. The Franciscan theologian Scotus differed somewhat from Aquinas' teaching as, definitively, did William of Ockham.[10] Ockham's view is usually called the 'Divine Command' theory. Catholic theology on the whole has followed Aquinas.

Vincent MacNamara memorably expresses the dominant tradition, therefore, when he writes that 'God is no more the author of the principles of morality than… of the principles of logic'. Plainly, it is not the case that God created humans and subsequently laid down, say, the principle of non-contradiction: in Aristotle's formulation, 'It is impossible for the same thing at the same time to belong and not belong to the same thing at the same time and in the same respect' – more simply (perhaps), it is logically impossible that something should be simultaneously true and false in the same respect.[11] Rather, granted the world which God created, and the human mind, and the meaning of the principle, the principle could not be other than true; and the human mind can see its truth.

So with morality. Though God is not the author of morality's rules in the crude sense which it is all too easy to take from some attempts to relate religion and morality, it by no means follows that God has no connection with morality at all. For the Bible teaches that God *is* the author of the creation, and has made humans in the divine likeness. It is in the creativity of the human being that the discovery of moral principle originates; but Christian theology sees that creativity as reflecting and indeed expressing the creativity of God. This is what St Thomas Aquinas had in mind when he wrote of natural law as a 'sharing in the Eternal Law by rational creatures'.[12]

Religion distorted

To see God and morality as related in a crudely legalistic way is in the first place to distort the God of Judaeo-Christian revelation. For although, viewed in a certain way, God may be regarded as a lawmaker, it cannot be on the model of the secular legislator of (for example) medieval Western experience, since the God of Moses and of Jesus Christ is a loving, merciful, compassionate, gracious God, whose way is the way of truth and of love. Right moral living is, as we shall see, an inescapable entailment of acceptance of the gospel of Jesus, but gospel precedes law and – to put it in Pauline terms – it is by the grace of God, and not by the Law, that we are saved.

Morality distorted

But when religion and morality are crudely related, morality also is distorted. Obedience to the moral law for fear of damnation or out of a desire to be rewarded is of the same order as the obedience of the child who fears the loss of the mother's love, or later the loss of peer approval. This, as we saw, is an infantile morality, if it can be called morality at all, and a morality which is unworthy of the reasoning and free being which is the human. Looking at it another way, one might recall that true morality requires not just externally correct behaviour but also the right attitude and disposition and motivation and intention. If these internal factors are corrupted, as when infected by un-adult and even inhuman influences, what ensues is not a human morality but a caricature.[13]

When the command of God is linked with promise of reward or threat of punishment, so that we obey out of fear or in hope of winning approval, our motivation too is debased. If we are moved to be just or truthful solely for fear of the consequences of acting otherwise, we have as it were missed the point of morality altogether. Truthfulness and justice have their own intrinsic worth, and they should be pursued for what they are worth in themselves. A view of morality which of its nature precludes our seeing them thus is a falsification.[14]

An account of morality in secular terms need not leave the Christian disquieted for it is the consequence of a deeply Christian theological insight.[15] It enhances morality by pointing up its intrinsic worth. But it also enhances religion, by freeing it to achieve its true depth and breadth. Of course, we should expect religious faith to have something to say to morality. For how we relate to the world and each other depends on what we make of life, and what we make of life is expressed in our 'faith' or other world-view. The Christian faith is a way of looking at life, and it is not surprising that as such it should have something to say about how we are to live. We shall shortly look in detail at what it says.

Notes

1   '...Buddhism in all its forms denies the existence of a transcendent creator-deity in favour of an indefinable, nonpersonal, absolute source or dimension that can be experienced as the depth of human inwardness. This, of course, is not to forget the multitudinous godlings, bodhisattvas, and spirits who are given ritual reverence in popular adaptations of the high religion to

human need.' M. Eliade (ed.), *The Encyclopedia of Religion*, New York and London, 1987, vol. 12, art. 'Religion'.

2   It has been suggested that the search for a definition of religion is primarily a Western concern, 'a natural consequence of the Western speculative, intellectualistic, and scientific disposition'; and also 'the product of the dominant Western religious mode, 'the theistic inheritance from Judaism, Christianity and Islam'. (ibid.). Needless to say, no disrespect is intended in the definition here attempted, where belief in a transcendent creator-deity is said to be 'commonly' an incident of religion.

3   There are, apparently, some: 'there are primitive societies in which there is no real connection between the ritual system, with its associated beliefs in supernatural beings, and the moral code'. *Encyclopedia of Philosophy*, ed. Paul Edwards, NewYork/London 1967, vol. 4, 140, art. 'Religion'. No examples are given.

4   Wrongly attributed perhaps, but it does summarise the attitude of Ivan in *The Brothers Karamazov*.

5   Kant's argument for the existence of God as a postulate of practical reason does not amount to a claim that the moral order proves the existence of God. For an interesting attempt to go further, see J.M. Rist, *Real Ethics: Rethinking the Foundations of Morality*, Cambridge 2002.

6   'This requirement of *interiority* [the *Catechism* continues] is all the more necessary as life often distracts us from any reflection, self-examination or introspection'.

7   *Gaudium et Spes* (Constitution on the Church in the Modern World), par 16. The translation used throughout this book is as in A. Flannery OP, *Vatican Council II: the Basic Sixteen Documents*, Dublin, 1996, hereinafter Fl.

8   Ibid.

9   Compare Seamus Heaney's *Docker*: 'Mosaic imperatives bang home like rivets;/God is a foreman with certain definite views', *Death of a Naturalist*, London/Boston, 1966.

10   The view taken by Aquinas is called 'intellectualism', that of Ockham 'voluntarism'. Philosophical versions of these views were argued in the seventeenth century by, respectively, Spinoza and Leibniz.

11   *Metaphysics*, 1005b12-20. Aristotle called this 'the most certain principle of all'.

12   *Summa Theologiae*, 1a 2ae, q 91, art 2. The translation used here is

that of the Blackfriars edition, volume 28, ed. Thomas Gilby OP, which contains Aquinas' so-called Tract on Law. The reference is to page 232.

13   Distortion of morality by 'religion' is vividly dramatised in Arthur Miller's *The Crucible*; and the distortion of both in some influential manuals of Catholic moral theology is – all too accurately – captured in the sermons on the Last Things, and especially the sermon on Hell, in James Joyce's *Portrait of the Artist as a Young Man*. A gentler and amusing, but no less accurate, insight into common attitudes to religion and morality among Catholics in the period just prior to the Second Vatican Council is found in David Lodge's *How Far Can You Go?*

14   Some writers have sought to state the Divine Command theory in such a way as to rescue it from the charge that it makes moral rules arbitrary and distorts morality beyond recognition: see Rist, op. cit., esp. 60-62.

15   Grace presupposes and enhances nature; faith is not at variance with reason.

7

Sources of Christian Moral Teaching

This book was earlier described as a reflection on morality in the light of Christian beliefs about humanity and the world, and the question now arises, where are those beliefs to be found?[1] An obvious place for Roman Catholics is the *Catechism of the Catholic Church* and, as it happens, the section of the *Catechism* which deals with this book's interests is especially clear and informative.[2] But of course there then arises the question, where did the *Catechism* get its teaching, what is the ultimate reference-point for Christian thinking about morality, what are the sources of moral theology?

If morality is the art of right relationship with others and with our world, it follows that anything which sheds light on what it is to be a human being is a potential source for reflecting on morality, and there are sources which the moral theologian shares with the moral philosopher. So, for example, psychology is an important locus, as are sociology and anthropology, and the older disciplines of history and law and medicine. So also are literature and the other arts; we have already seen how conscience may be educated through a play or a film or novel or poem.

Tradition
There are, however, sources which are specific to moral theology, which speak directly of and to the beliefs and

practices of the Christian community, and these are usually referred to as scripture and tradition. The tradition in question is the tradition of the believing community, and it may be useful if we invert the usual order and consider it first, since the scriptures themselves reflect the tradition of the community. Tradition is *what* is handed on and the *manner* of handing on – both content and the process – and the biblical books document the impact of the disclosure of God in the affairs of the people of Israel and then in the personal history of Jesus Christ.

What is handed on in the Christian tradition is a living faith, and it is handed on in the *practice* of Christians, in the way in which they live life, in the institutions in which Christian beliefs are embodied, in the rituals and symbols by which Christian faith is expressed. The tradition is therefore in the first place a *living* reality, and its values and meanings are 'caught' as much as 'taught', as is sometimes said of the appropriation of literature. But what is written has a special importance, and so the documents of the tradition are an essential resource.

As already said, the scriptures are, as it were, the first documents of the tradition, holding a unique place, and we shall look at their significance closely soon. Subsequent documents, however, also reflect the unfolding reality of 'life in Christ' and as such have their own importance. They are numerous and varied, ranging from treatises and sermons by key figures in the life of the early Church (for example St Augustine), through the work of the theologians of the Middle Ages (St Thomas Aquinas is the dominant figure), to the leading theologians and Church men and women of the Reformation and modern periods. Especially authoritative – ultimately and decisively, one might say – are the Creeds and other enactments of the great Councils (the Nicene Creed, for example), or the decrees of the Council of Trent in the sixteenth century, or of the Vatican Councils of the nineteenth and twentieth; and of course the teachings of the popes.

How to interpret the tradition is obviously an important question, and especially so is the question of how the moral teaching of the Bible might apply to us now. In a moment we shall focus on this latter question, but some points applicable also to the other documents may first be made.

Respect for tradition is an elementary prerequisite of any search for knowledge and truth; we know what we know – in science, in law, in the humanities, in technology – in the first place because of what our forebears have handed on. When Einstein established his Theory of Relativity, and Heisenberg the Indeterminacy Principle, they were changing accepted physics theory, modifying what had been taught since Newton. But neither could have made his contribution unless Newton had first made his, and unless they had submitted themselves to the tradition inaugurated by Newton's work.

Yet respect for tradition cannot mean merely repeating what has been handed on, as indeed these examples show; and what is true for physics is true, *mutatis mutandis*, for morality too. New problems arise about which the tradition is silent: neither the Bible nor the writings of Church Fathers or of medieval theologians have anything to tell us about computer ethics. Alternatively, old problems present themselves in a new light; a doctrine of the ethics of warfare conceived when warfare took place between combatants on a battle-field obviously needs revision in an age when weapons of mass destruction render a distinction between combatant and non-combatant practically pointless.

We might also discover that it would be simply wrong (and not just inept) to repeat what has been handed on: attempts to justify slavery by reference to Paul's teaching about the duties of slaves and masters[3] were wrong – as is any attempt to teach a subordination of women by reference to what he has to say about husbands and wives.[4] The Christian tradition sanctioned capital punishment; many Christians today – including Pope John Paul II – consider it immoral. What was handed on in the

Catholic Church concerning religious freedom was found
wanting by the Second Vatican Council, whose teaching in the
Declaration on Religious Freedom is a definite break with the
tradition.

Magisterium

In virtue of baptism each Christian is called to hand on the
faith, and in our time theology is especially alive to the vocation
of each member of the believing community. Yet it is also true
that in the Roman Catholic tradition a special and ultimate
responsibility rests with the pope and the bishops, whose
magisterium or teaching role is inherent in the service which
they are appointed to provide to the gospel and to the
community called Church.[5]

Again, the topic of authority in the Church, including
teaching authority, cannot be examined in detail here. Suffice it
to say that the tradition claims for the holders of *magisterium* a
teaching role in moral matters[6] – unsurprisingly, for the gospel
has implications for how Christians are to live. Of this teaching
role the *Catechism* says: 'The Magisterium of the Pastors of the
Church in moral matters is ordinarily exercised in catechesis
and preaching, with the help of the work of theologians and
spiritual authors. Thus, from generation to generation, under
the aegis and vigilance of the pastors, the "deposit" of
Christian moral teaching has been handed on, a deposit
composed of a characteristic body of rules, commandments
and virtues proceeding from faith in Christ and animated by
charity. Alongside the Creed and the Our Father, the basis for
this catechesis has traditionally been the Decalogue which sets
out the principles of moral life valid for all men' (*CCC*, 2033).

Which brings us conveniently to the Bible and its singular
status among the documents of the tradition. The Bible is for
Christians the Word of God and, as is explained elsewhere in
this series, Christian thinking generally characterises it as
'inspired', as did Judaism the Hebrew Bible. Hence the Bible is

par excellence the source and reference-point for all Christian theology.[7]

What to expect from the Bible

What then has the Bible to say about morality? It is obvious that it is not a text-book in moral theology or a comprehensive ethical code. A text-book is a more or less systematic introduction to or summary of its subject-matter; it proceeds in an organised way, aiming to be comprehensive and up to date. A glance at the biblical books is enough to show that they are simply not this sort of book, individually or taken together. The moral teaching of the biblical books is on the whole incidental and occasional, arising in the course of a narrative or story about other, 'larger', matters.

Thus the Decalogue occurs in the course of the story of the Covenant between God and the Israelites made with Moses, itself part of a larger story, that of the promise made by God to Abraham and his descendants of a great and glorious destiny. There is moral teaching and preaching in the writings of prophets such as Isaiah or Jeremiah, but it occurs in the course of a narrative which has to do with how the people have been responding to God's promise and covenant, and it usually has to do with reminding them that they cannot say they love God if they do not love their neighbour. In the New Testament, as we shall see, the moral teaching of Jesus is embedded in a narrative or narratives about who Jesus was and what he did; and the ethical content – the rules for living – of the other books is consequent upon their teaching about Jesus, and about God's dealings with humanity as incarnated in Jesus' person and history.

So the moral teaching of the Bible is not systematic or organised; and neither is it comprehensive, in the sense of offering a detailed code of conduct valid for every time and place. Biblical teaching says nothing about computer ethics or about the problems which arise from modern advances in science. It does not answer the question whether or not it is right to modify crops or food in the ways now open to modern biotechnology. It says nothing about whether it is right or wrong to turn off a respirator when that is all that is keeping a patient alive who must otherwise certainly die. There are many moral problems upon which the Bible sheds no light, or at least not directly, for the simple reason that these problems didn't exist when the books were written.

There are also moral imperatives in biblical books which have no force now. Paul's teaching about the mutual duties of slaves and masters are obsolete for a mentality for which the institution of slavery is immoral. His injunction not to indulge in litigation is not followed absolutely (even if in our litigious time we might do well to take more notice of it than we do). His teaching about the relationships between husbands and wives would, to say the least of it, need to be reformulated in a world more attuned to gender equality than his was.[8]

Interpretation and appropriation

How then are we to understand the Bible's moral teaching? Scholars speak of a two-fold task, interpretation and appropriation. If we are to *apply* 'what the Bible says' to our own ethical concerns, we must first do our best to *establish* what the Bible says. This latter task involves trying to discover what a biblical writer *understood himself to be saying.* 'There are two distinct steps, therefore, in any attempt to apply biblical material in Christian ethics: interpretation of biblical texts and some kind of appropriation or contemporization'[9].

T. Deidun observes that many modern scholars insist that these steps are not in fact distinguishable, that 'the merging of the interpreter's horizons with those of the text is integral to any act of interpretation'[10], that exegesis is – and should be – 'engaged'. Yet as a first step he himself opts for what is called the historical-critical method, or cluster of methods, which 'operates on the principle that a prerequisite for discovering what any given biblical writer understood himself to be saying is a careful use of all available critical tools (historical, linguistic and literary), joined with an honest effort to be objective and an openness to unfamiliar ideas'[11]. For, as he puts it, 'experience surely teaches us (if common sense failed to do so) that interpreters who turn to biblical texts in search of "relevance" will surely find what they are looking for, but only after imposing on the texts their own notions of what counts as relevance'[12].

Biblical interpretation according to Vatican II

The above statement is consistent with what the Second Vatican Council affirmed regarding the interpretation of Scripture, and one way of approaching our own question is to start from what the Council said. This is found in chapter three – and especially in paragraph twelve – of the Constitution on Divine Revelation, *Dei Verbum*. I shall take the various elements in order, but it will help if we keep in mind that the central idea is this: in the Bible God speaks to us in the words of the writers, and if we want to know what God intends to say, we must find out what the writer intended to say. As the Council puts it: 'Seeing that, in sacred scripture, God speaks through human beings in human fashion, it follows that the interpreters of sacred scripture, if they are to ascertain what God has wished to communicate to us, should carefully search out the meaning which the sacred writers really had in mind....'[13]

But how do we know what the writers 'really had in mind'? A preliminary answer is that '[i]n determining the intention of the sacred writers, attention must be paid, among other things, to *literary genres*.' This is not surprising: we don't read a novel as if it were a history book, or science fiction as if it were science; and we know that when Keats wrote 'I cannot see what flowers are at my feet/Nor what soft incense hangs upon the bough', he wasn't saying that incense grows on trees. 'The fact is that truth is differently presented and expressed in the various types of historical writing, in prophetical and poetical texts, and in other forms of literary expression. Hence the exegete must look for that meaning which the sacred writers ... intended to express and did in fact express through the medium of a contemporary literary form.'

Another requirement is that one pays attention to context – the literary context of course, but also the socio-cultural context out of which the book emerged. It would violate an elementary rule of interpretation were one to pluck a sentence out of the paragraph in which it occurs, without regard to the relationship of the sentence to the rest of the piece. But it would also be a mistake to try to interpret any work from the past without reference to the milieu in which it was produced. This is what the Council means when it says that we should look for the meaning which the writers intended 'in given situations and granted the circumstances of their time and culture'.

Finally the Council says that 'due attention must be paid both to the customary and characteristic patterns of perception, speech and narrative which prevailed in their time, and to the conventions which people then observed in their dealings with one another.'

Attention to patterns of perception will involve our not assuming that the Bible's authors saw things as we do: consider the differences between our sense of when and how the world might end and theirs.[14] As to customary and characteristic patterns of speech and narrative, one has to bear in mind for example that the biblical writings came out of an oral tradition, and that the books reflect this in such devices as parallelism, various mnemonic devices, hyperbole and paradox. Also important is what one writer has described as 'a constellation of figurative forms': Jesus' teaching in particular contained a variety of linguistic elements – proverbs, riddles, aphorisms, allegories, analogies, parables, and so on.[15]

The foregoing should be enough to indicate the care which must be taken when looking in scripture for teaching intended to illuminate current ethical problems, and especially if this amounts to a search for timeless and immutable norms. There are such norms in the sacred text; but they are not such simply because they are in the sacred text, but rather because they are the kind of norm which *can* be timeless. So, for example, the commandment to love thy neighbour, or the injunction to be just or truthful or compassionate or humble, are in the Christian view rightly considered immutable and timeless, as is the prohibition of murder or adultery or perjury. By the same token, a norm which in itself cannot be timeless and immutable is not made so by being in the Bible: a prohibition on litigation, for example, or on oath-taking is not given the status of a universal principle through being taught by Paul.

Vision

It is latterly suggested by scholars that to search only for norms and principles is to run the risk of missing what the biblical books have to offer by way of light on the moral life. And that is in the first place a vision of life, a vision of what it is to be human, and of what the destiny of humans and their world is, and how a people can grow in relationship with their God. So it is that attention to the grand theological themes is called for: creation, sin, redemption, grace, salvation. In the Bible these are not doctrinal abstractions but theology-laden 'events' whose meaning is unfolded in the narrative or narratives which constitute the Bible's story. So it is also that in seeking the ethical message of Jesus we must look first at his 'gospel', for this is his primary message, and only when we have taken it in can we understand the call to 'come, follow me'.

Notes

1   It is theologically more accurate to describe moral theology as a reflection in the light of Christian faith or of revelation, but an explanation of these concepts would take us too far afield, and our purposes are adequately served by the description adopted.

2   See Part Three, 'Life in Christ', especially Section One.

3   Eph. 6:5-10.

4   Eph. 5:21 ff. Scholars are recently observing that what Paul says about both marriage and slavery is in fact an advance on what was customary in the culture, for he thinks of all relationships as transformed 'in Christ', so that class and other distinctions are abolished.

5   See *Lumen Gentium* (Constitution on the Church), chapter 3. Fl 25ff.

6   See *Catechism of the Catholic Church*, Part Three, Section One, chapter three, article three, 'Moral Life and the Magisterium of the Church', and references. Standard works in theology of *magisterium* generally are Francis A. Sullivan, *Magisterium, Teaching Authority in the Catholic Church*, Dublin, 1983, and his *Creative Fidelity: Weighing and Interpreting Church Documents*, New York/Mahwah, 1996.

7   The use of the Bible in question here is as a source for theology; its devotional use, as in *lectio divina* or other forms of meditation and prayer, is a separate matter.

8   But see n.3 above

9   T. Deidun, 'The Bible and Christian Ethics', in B. Hoose (ed.), *Christian Ethics: an Introduction*, London, 1998, 4. This article summarises other approaches; and see also W. Spohn, *What Are They Saying About Scripture and Ethics?* Revised Edition, New York, 1995.

10   Ibid.

11   Deidun in Hoose op. cit. 5. See also J. Barton, 'Historical-Critical Approaches', in J. Barton (ed.), *Biblical Interpretation*, Cambridge, 1998, 9-20. The Pontifical Biblical Commission considers that '[t]the historical-critical method is the indispensable method for the scientific study of the meaning of ancient texts', and that to attempt to bypass it would be 'to create an illusion'; Section 1 A and Conclusion. (Full text found at http://www.ewtn.com/library/CURIA/PBCINTER .HTM.) This is not to deny the validity of other approaches, only to indicate that, if not grounded in historico-critical work, they may result in a scholar's imposing prejudices upon the text.

12   Ibid.

13   Par 12. This and subsequent quotations in the chapter are from Fl.
     105-106.

14   A simple illustration of the force of this point, even if not directly
     relevant, is in the fact that the people of the Bible, like other
     ancient peoples, thought that the earth was flat.

15   T.H. McLaughlin (2004), 'Nicholas Burbules on Jesus as Teacher' in
     Hanan Alexander (ed.), *Spirituality and Ethics in Education:
     Philosophical, Theological and Radical Perspectives*, Brighton, 2004, 21-
     33.

8

Gospel and Law

Jesus Christ

The Christian religion is founded upon the belief that God is disclosed uniquely in Jesus Christ. According to a modern theological emphasis, that disclosure took place in the personal *history* of Jesus. As the Constitution on Revelation of the Second Vatican Council has it, Jesus revealed God 'by the total fact of his presence and self-manifestation – by words and works, signs and miracles, but above all by his death and glorious resurrection from the dead, and finally by sending the Spirit of truth'.[1] What this means is that God is disclosed, and God's design for the creation, in the detail of the personal history of Jesus.

That history itself took place within the history of a people who had already experienced themselves as especially chosen. God, they believed, was being revealed in the unfolding story of their 'deliverance', in accordance with a promise made to Abraham and ratified in a covenant with Moses. Although their expectations were in time no longer crassly political, most of his hearers were unprepared for the claim that their deliverance was less from temporal enemies and evils than from the bondage of sin, and that their saviour was a travelling rabbi from Nazareth who said he was the Son of God.

So they crucified him, but 'God raised him up',[2] and later he was seen by some of the disciples.[3] Later again they came to recognise that he had left them definitively and had gone back to the Father.[4] What then came to be called the Church was born in the coming together of Jesus' disciples, following his injunction to remember in the breaking of bread[5] what he had done, or rather what God had done in him. The core of the disciples' belief was that Jesus was Lord, who had died and was risen and would some time come again. They were at first fearful and inhibited but, transformed by the Pentecost event, at length went forth to tell others of their faith and hope.[6]

Gospel

Their message was called 'good news' – the Greek *euangelion* and the English 'gospel' have comparable roots. In classical Greek the term was often used in reference to the announcement of a victory, and in fact it was still used in New Testament times to refer to the victory of the emperor. But in a religious context it could signify a divine utterance, and perhaps the sense in which the expression came most readily to the disciples was a strictly biblical one: it echoed exactly a word used in Second Isaiah to signify that the time of salvation was at hand.

Salvation was a familiar theme in the religious patrimony of Israel. The complex history of the theme is beyond our purpose; essentially the concept signified the action of God in the life of the chosen people, in virtue of which they were to achieve the destiny promised to the descendants of Abraham. The shape of that destiny disclosed itself only gradually, and only gradually did it come to be associated with the expectation of a messiah. But by the time of the prophets it had begun to appear that salvation was not to be an event in the political order only, and the saviour was seen in the role of a suffering Servant.[7]

This was the backdrop to the events that are the subject of the narratives which we now call gospels. These books, each from its own viewpoint, document the impact of Jesus of Nazareth upon his hearers. They tell the story of Jesus, a story which was perceived by himself and by those who became his disciples as continuing and completing the story of God's dealings with the people of God's choice.

Luke, therefore, portrays Jesus, early in his public ministry, announcing in the synagogue at Nazareth that the words of the prophet Isaiah were in him that day fulfilled: 'The Spirit of the Lord is upon me, because he has anointed me to preach good news to the poor. He has sent me to proclaim release to the captives and recovering of sight to the blind, to set at liberty those who are oppressed, to proclaim the acceptable year of the Lord'.[8] That *this* is the salvation that Israel was waiting for was a main theme in the spreading of the good news.

It seems that a brief telling of the story of Jesus was a central feature of the early proclamation of the gospel. Several of Paul's letters and some passages in the Acts of the Apostles incorporate such a narrative, and Peter's speech to Cornelius as reported in Acts will serve to exemplify this here:

> You know the word which [God] sent to Israel, preaching the good news of peace by Jesus Christ (he is Lord of all), the word which was proclaimed throughout all Judea, beginning from Galilee after the baptism which John preached: how God anointed Jesus of Nazareth with the Holy Spirit and with power; how he went about doing good and healing all that were oppressed by the devil, for God was with him. And we are witnesses to all that he did both in the country of the Jews and in Jerusalem. They put him to death by hanging him on a tree; but God raised him up on the third day and made him manifest; not to all the people but to us who were chosen by God as witnesses, who ate and drank with him after he rose from the dead. And he commanded us to preach to the people, and to testify that he is the one ordained

by the Lord to be judge of the living and the dead. To
him all the prophets bear witness that everyone who
believes in him receives forgiveness of sins through his
name.[9]

Church and morality

We therefore have a community – or, more exactly, communities
– gathering in remembrance of the story of Jesus' life, and
especially in what would become known as the paschal events;
and then going out to spread the word that in him is salvation
accomplished. It took a little time before it was clear that
subscription to that Jewish tradition was not a prerequisite of
entry into the Christian 'way', somewhat longer before the new
'churches' realised their distinctiveness in the common Jewish
tradition. It took yet longer before their community of faith
and worship generated a community of organisation: before,
that is, the churches became the Church, which in time would
be one in government as well as in worship and faith.

From the outset, however, the churches saw themselves as
charged with proclaiming the good news. The disciples were
conscious of being 'sent', as Peter's speech just quoted shows.
Matthew records a sending,[10] and later he presents the risen
Lord on a mountain in Galilee bidding the eleven 'go and make
disciples of all nations, baptising them in the name of the
Father and of the Son and of the Holy Spirit, teaching them to
observe all that I have commanded you'.[11]

It is a commonplace of modern ecclesiology that the
Church 'is mission' – so much a commonplace that one is
tempted to try to find another way of saying what is meant. Yet
there is hardly a more exact way of saying that in its very
coming together to celebrate Jesus as Lord it is meant to go
forth to affirm what it celebrates. 'As the Father has sent me I
also send you'.[12] In a later theological perspective the Church
would be seen as a visible expression in history of the saving
work of Christ.

Thus, very summarily, the emergence of the community of believers in the risen Lord which we call Church; and now it is time to turn to what they made of morality. The Christian religion, in a well-known dictum of C.H. Dodd, 'is an ethical religion in the specific sense that it recognises no ultimate separation between the service of God and social behaviour'.[13] What this means is that you cannot claim to love the God of Jesus Christ unless you love the neighbour. Of course, the link between religion and morality had already been affirmed in Judaism, and there was much in the tradition inherited by the first Christians to remind them of it. V. Warnach has summarised the data: 'In the Old Testament the love which God bestows upon men, above all on the chosen people, is for the most part understood as faithfulness to the covenant. In view of this it is not surprising that the reciprocal love of men should likewise be conceived of as consisting essentially in the acceptance of covenant obligations'.[14]

These obligations included worship; but no less did they stress the need for a right relationship with the neighbour. Indeed, it was to be a constant theme, especially in the preaching of the prophets, that the God of Israel was not placated by mere ritual in the absence of a conversion of heart expressed in right conduct toward others.[15]

The Kingdom of God and repentance

Following on from the reasoning above, it was not, as it were, out of the blue that Jesus preached repentance. 'Repentance' translates a Greek word *metanoia* which is richer in its signification than the English. Its chief Old Testament antecedent is a Hebrew word *shuv*, whose literal meaning is to return to the place from which one has set out, that is, to God. When Jesus calls for repentance he is calling on people to turn about, to reorient their lives, to make a fresh beginning, to go back to God.[16]

Yet the call to repentance was not the primary motif of the message; that motif was, rather, the coming of the kingdom of God. Again we need to be careful of the English word: 'kingship' or 'reign' or 'rule' are better guides to the biblical sense. For in the tradition God had often been thought of as king, and in time the hope of Israel was expressed in terms of the setting up of God's kingly rule in Israel and among the nations.[17]

The rule would not, however, be a merely political dominion. Isaiah's vision of it is summarised by Rudolph Schnackenburg: 'The peace of paradise will be brought back (Is 11:6-9), and, in general, this kingdom of God fulfilled in the last age takes on universal characteristics even though Israel has always the place of honour. It also has cosmic dimensions and a clearly religious and moral character – salvation and peace and the law established as the basis of the world order'.[18] It will simplify matters if we indicate its meaning by calling it the universal reign of God's love.

In Jesus' preaching the advent of that reign is the context of the call to repentance. Mark's portrayal of the opening of the public ministry shows this: 'The time is fulfilled and the kingdom of God is at hand; repent and believe in the gospel'.[19] The time of the promise is here, the rule of God's love is inaugurated, and the people are called to turn again to him. The turning implies a change of heart, and the change is expressed in walking along the right path. But the turning is in another sense only like a first move, a step within a larger process. For Jesus asks them also to believe the gospel or believe in it, to entrust themselves to the word that God has saved God's people. They are invited to recognise their salvation *and then* walk in salvation's way.

The call to repentance, therefore, is at root a call to acknowledge the presence of God's love and its power. To see it merely as a summons to moral rectitude is to impoverish it. What is announced first is that God loves us, and in that very announcement we are asked to return that love. If we want to return it we are thereby committed to love of the neighbour. In the gospel accounts, as a glance will show, Jesus repeatedly reiterates the love-commandment and places it at the heart of the religious and moral response which he asks of his disciples.[20]

It is, however, important to remember that Jesus was not primarily a moral teacher. True, as we have seen, what he taught had a bearing on morality, and he did sometimes teach morality directly: the primacy of the love-commandment, the scope and quality of the love which it enjoins, something of what it precludes as well as what it asks to be done. As with the call to repentance, however, the moral teaching of Jesus is consequent upon his gospel. It opens up the path of love for one in whom God's love has resonated.

The Gospel as a new way of living

The first hearers grasped these ideas well, and this is reflected in the way they shaped their own teaching. First they announced the good news, as had Jesus in announcing the coming of the kingdom; then they explained what this meant in terms of the expectations and preoccupations of Jew or Gentile as the context called for; and then they bade the new disciples to 'let your manner of life be worthy of the gospel of Christ'.[21] Sometimes too they gave specific indications of the kind of behaviour which this required: see, for example, Romans 12, 13; 1 Corinthians 5-8. But always the concrete moral instruction – the normative ethic – was consequent upon the announcement of the gospel.

Biblical scholarship furnishes a terminology for analysing the approach which the first Christian preachers adopted. The statement of the essence of the good news is called *kerygma*, a word which means the message of a herald and so is suitable in reference to the *euangelion*. Jesus' own *kerygma*, we have seen, was characteristically expressed in terms of the coming of

God's reign, explicitly or implicitly identified with his own presence. That formula or some version of it featured too in the spreading of the good news by the disciples; and as we saw in Peter's speech to Cornelius its link with Jesus was made by a recital of the main events of his life, with special emphasis on the death and resurrection. What the first preachers were intent above all to convey was that Jesus is the Christ, Son of God, so that their hearers, believing, might have life in his name.[22]

The preaching of the *kerygma*, however, inevitably gave rise to a need for explanation, called by the scholars *catechesis*; and this assumed a typical shape at an early stage.[23] Our interest is in its ethical component, called *Didache*, a word which meant teaching – in this context moral instruction. Another biblical term for it is *paraenesis*, meaning, literally, moral exhortation.

I have been stressing that in Jesus' teaching moral instruction must be seen in the context of his proclamation of God's reign. The same point is made in the way in which the moral teaching in the four Gospels is set within a narrative which presents Jesus as inaugurating that reign. The subordination of moral instruction to religious message is, however, perhaps most clearly seen in the structure of the Pauline and other New Testament Letters.[24] The Letter to the Romans will serve as an example.

The Letter to the Romans is 'the record of the maturing thoughts of Paul, written on the occasion of his impending visit to Rome, in which he formulated the more universal implications of the gospel which he had been preaching'.[25] Paul first considers the way in which God, through Christ, 'justifies' the person of faith. He goes on to show how God's love assures salvation to all thus justified, paying special attention to the three-fold liberation which life 'in Christ' brings: freedom from sin and death, freedom from self through union with Christ, and freedom from the Law. The role of the Spirit in this new life is explored, as is the Christian's destiny in 'glory'. The reflections conclude with a paean: 'O the depth of the riches and wisdom and knowledge of God! How unsearchable his judgments and how inscrutable his ways! For from him and through him and to him are all things. To him be glory for ever. Amen'.[26] Only then does Paul turn to moral exhortation.

Moral exhortation in the New Testament

I chose the Letter to the Romans to illustrate the structure of which we have been speaking – the pattern which makes moral *didache* subordinate to the affirmations of the *kerygma* – for in that letter the pattern is seen at its plainest. But the structure may be detected in other New Testament letters too, as theological reflection – often in a mood of thanksgiving or of celebration – leads on to exhortation about good living. We must now look, summarily, at the exhortation's content.[27]

At its core is the notion that the Christian convert is to turn from sinful ways and to live a life of virtue, 'to put off the old man and to put on the new', as it is sometimes expressed. The vices which must be laid aside are enumerated, and some typical virtues are set out – purity, sobriety, gentleness, humility, generosity, patience, and a readiness to forgive. It is plain that the 'change of heart' (*metanoia*) was meant to affect day-to-day living and to permeate it through and through. The ambit of that living was manifold: the family and other domestic relations, the larger community of Christians, pagan neighbours, the civil authority. No part of life is untouched by the new experience of faith in Jesus Christ, and all of living is somehow judged by it.

The New Testament writings show that the new experience suffused the view of life of the first hearers, and the developing Christian imagination sought ways in which to express the sense of newness engendered by the gospel. And so the early writers spoke of dying and rising with Christ, a second birth, adoption into the family of God's children, putting on the new man. 'The radicality of the metaphors bespeaks a real experience of sharp displacement which many of the converts must have felt'.[28] The first Christians are no longer at ease here, like Eliot's Magi after the birth.[29]

Notes

1   *Dei Verbum*, par 4. Fl 98-99.
2   Acts 2:24. The translation used in this book is that of the Revised Standard Version.
3   Mk 16 and parallels.
4   Mk 16:19.
5   Lk 22:19; cf 1Cor 11:23-26.
6   Acts 7.
7   Is 42.
8   Lk 4:18,19.
9   Acts 11:36-43.
10   Mt 10:5 ff.
11   Mt 28:19, 20.
12   Jn 20:21.
13   *Gospel and Law*, New York, 1951, 13.
14   In Bauer (ed.), *Encyclopedia of Biblical Theology*, London, 1976, art. 'Love', 522-3.
15   See for example Isaiah 1.
16   See Bauer, op. cit., art. 'Conversion'.
17   Ibid., art. 'Kingdom of God'.
18   In Bauer, ibid.
19   Mk 1:15.
20   Mt 22:23-40, Mk 12:28-34, Lk 10:25 ff.
21   Phil 1:27.
22   Jn 20:31
23   For an account see, for example, A. Robert and A. Tricot, *Guide to the Bible*, vol 1, Paris, 1963.
24   To speak of subordination is not meant to imply that the Bible makes little of morality; on the contrary and clearly, all the documents envisage good living as an integral part of response to God. The point I wish to bring out is that the response is begotten of the proclamation first of the gospel; in evangelisation one doesn't as it were skip to the ethics.

25   J.A. Fitzmyer, SJ, 'The Letter to the Romans', *The New Jerome Biblical Commentary*, ed. Brown, Fitzmyer and Murphy, Englewood Cliffs N.J., 1990, 830.

26   Rom 11:33-36.

27   What follows is based on Dodd, *Gospel and Law*, 17 ff.

28   Wayne Meeks, *The Moral World of the First Christians*, London, 1987, 13. Meeks' *The Origins of Christian Morality; the First Two Centuries*, New Haven and London, 1993, is also illuminating.

29   T.S. Eliot, 'Journey of the Magi', *Collected Poems 1909-1962*, London, 1974.

9

Christian Faith and Morality

The last chapter spoke of a sense of 'displacement' in the first Christians, revealed in the various metaphors by which Paul and others tried to express life under the gospel: dying and rising with Christ, a second birth, adoption, putting on the new man, and so on. And yet there is an ordinariness about the imperatives of the earliest instruction, a kind of modesty which keeps it earthbound. The vices condemned are those which any sound ethic might condemn, the virtues by and large are of a kind aspired to by anyone wishing to live humanely. Christians are not to be conformed to this world,[1] Paul wrote; yet, as one commentator has put it, 'his typical admonitions, which follow those words, are sprinkled with topics and turns of phrase that would be instantly recognisable in the moral rhetoric of his time and place'.[2] Scholars have long acknowledged that the early writers made use of existing ethical writing in setting out the demands of the Christian way of life.

The early Christian writers, of course, were able to draw on a wealth of ethical wisdom from more than one tradition. There was in the first place the Jewish tradition, which formed Jesus himself, and was the background to the first post-Pentecost spreading of the gospel in the Jewish homeland and in the diaspora. Then there was the moral content of the

Graeco-Roman heritage, a natural resource for those who like Paul took the message to the chief cities of the empire. Not that the Christian way was simply identical with that of Israel; and before long that point was tested in the controversy over circumcising gentile converts. Nor that, for example, the detachment from the world prized by the Christians was in the same spirit as that espoused by some Stoic philosophers. Yet it was from the moral perceptions of Israel and Athens and Rome that the earliest Christians fashioned their 'way'.

Wayne Meeks has expressed the foregoing in these words:

> The meaningful world in which those earliest Christians lived – the world which lived in their heads as well as that which was all around them – was a Jewish world. But the Jewish world was part of the Graeco-Roman world. If therefore we are looking for some 'pure' Christian values and beliefs unmixed with the surrounding culture, we are on a fool's errand. What was Christian about the ethos and ethics of those early Christian communities we will discover not by abstraction but by confronting their involvement in the culture of their time and place and seeking to trace the new patterns they made of old forms, to hear the new songs they composed from old melodies.[3]

Rather than looking for their adoption of norms of behaviour, therefore, which are different from those available in the current ethical wisdom, we should look to what they did with the wisdom – Jewish, Greek, Roman – at their disposal, and see how they re-envisaged living in the world 'in Christ'. What was distinctive about the way of the disciple? Meeks' words serve to warn against the danger of imposing an alien schema upon a process so complex as has been here sketched. Yet it happens that a modern theological debate offers one way of coping with the question. That debate concerns the precise

CHRISTIAN FAITH AND MORALITY   113

character, or, as it is sometimes called, the identity, of Christian morality. In view of the account of morality with which we have been working, the way in which the question arises might be put as follows. If morality is a matter of general human experience and if its prescriptions are accessible to reason, what role does Christian faith play? The question is often put in the form, is there a specifically Christian morality?

What was new?
Here we can only try to simplify a complex debate, and this account is based in the main upon the Roman Catholic experience of the question. In that experience the debate began when moral theologians, critical of accounts of Christian ethics which scarcely referred to Christ or to Christian sources, called for a return to the Bible as the source-book of all Christian theologising. There ensued a recovery of focus on the person and teaching of Jesus; and his emphasis on the love-commandment was taken to be the essential mark of any account of morality that wished to be Christian.

But what *was* this love? It was soon seen that in order to give concrete content to the love-commandment one needed to have recourse to specific prescriptions such as those of the Decalogue, and of the ethical teaching of the gospels and other New Testament books. And so love of neighbour was seen to be expressed in concrete norms: negative, as in prohibitions on killing, say, or stealing or lying or adultery; positive, in injunctions to be just or peaceful or truthful, or whatever the particular virtue or action.

A new kind of question then suggested itself however. Are not these precepts of peace and justice and respect for life and truthfulness, whether positively or negatively expressed, necessary to anyone who thinks about the prerequisites of a good life? The emergence of this type of question was influenced in great part by the work of Scripture scholars who were finding parallels between the moral teaching of the

Scriptures and that from other religious and even secular sources. It was noted, for example, that the main provisions of the Decalogue were the same, if differently formulated, as those of the Babylonian Code of Hammurabi. In addition, I have already alluded to Paul's use of stoic ethics, and mentioned the secular origins of other parts of the early Christian ethic. Such scholarly findings gave point to the question, is there anything in the moral teaching of the Bible, even of Jesus himself, that is not available to reason reflecting on human experience in the world?

Two approaches

The two lines of response which this question evoked have been called respectively the 'Autonomy' and *Glaubensethik* approaches. Proponents of the former are so called from the apparent autonomy which they attribute to morality vis-à-vis religion, though, as we shall see, the autonomy is relative, not absolute – they do *not* say that Christian faith has nothing to say to morality. The latter school gets its name from the German word for faith, and the name implies a view of Christian morality which connects it intimately with Christian belief. One of the ways in which the issue is often formulated is whether or to what extent 'revelation' is necessary to morality.

In answering this question the writers of the Autonomy school are in general reluctant to say that the revelation made in Jesus Christ has contributed anything to our knowledge of morality's *content*. Another way of putting this is to say that one doesn't need Christian faith in order to know *what* morality requires. These writers concede that revelation and faith give a *context* to moral striving, as the Covenant gave a context to the Israelites' keeping the Torah. In the terminology which we ourselves used when talking of religion and morality, these writers say that what faith supplied is a *vision of life* which informs our perceptions and choices. Most grant that this vision gives additional *motivation* for right behaviour: we love the neighbour for him/herself but also as sister or brother in the Lord. And of course the Christian has, in the person of Jesus, a *model* and *inspiration* for moral endeavour. But what to do or refrain from doing, in the cause of justice or respect for life or any other moral value, is, they say, in its substance the same for everyone 'of good will'.

Writers in the *Glaubensethik* school agree with the autonomists concerning context and motivation and the exemplary significance of Jesus. Where they disagree is on the question of content, for they maintain that in the Christian moral way there are some requirements whose existence and character and binding force are known only because of revelation. Of course the substance of morality's claims are accessible to reason, they acknowledge, and so are shared by all people of good will, but in the *Glaubensethik* view it is nevertheless the case that there are things asked of Christians which are recognised only in faith.

It is important to notice at this point that there are two versions of the *Glaubensethik* position, called respectively by commentators the strong and the weak. The strong is that there are *specific norms* available only through revelation and known in faith. The weaker form is that even if there are no specifically different norms, the Christian faith so shapes attitudes and activities that Christians will sometimes find themselves making choices which are more than 'merely reasonable', as when, for example, one 'goes the second mile' or 'turns the other cheek' – images of the generosity and radicality of the response asked of the disciple.

One might think that the question whether there are specific moral norms that are proper to Christianity is a question of fact which could be settled by recourse to the sources of revelation. One might expect, that is, that the *Glaubensethik* authors could provide a list of moral demands which are known only from Scripture and/or from the tradition of the Church, and which cannot be perceived as obligatory by the use of reason uninformed by Christian faith. If they can do this, one might think, their position is vindicated; if not, the autonomists have it.

The matter, however, is not so simple. The authors of the *Glaubensethik* do indeed provide a list (or lists, for they differ a little between themselves),[4] but the autonomists respond by contending that some of the items on the list are instances of religious rather than moral obligation, while others are taught in the Catholic tradition as grounded in reason as much as they are in revelation.

It may be observed that there is little to choose between the weaker form of the *Glaubensethik* approach and that of most autonomists. In order to decide between the stronger form and the autonomy thesis, however, we should have to agree in the first place upon the respective scopes of religion and morality, and to consider the import of the tradition's grounding of positions in revelation as well as in reason. We should also, as Vincent MacNamara has done, analyse each side's use of such terms as 'content' and 'motivation'. This task is too vast in the present context, however, and we must be content with a sketch of a working position.

The makings of a response

We might begin by recalling the incontrovertible. It is incontrovertible that the Judaeo-Christian theological inheritance provides a context in which the moral pilgrimage of humanity may be seen in a way that enhances it. There is the doctrine of creation, with its view of humans as made in the image of God and therefore called to take part in the very making of the world. There is the theme of human stewardship of creation, suggestive of an accountability for what is in our power and charge. Then there is the doctrine of sin, the 'sin of the world' and personal sin, a dark shadow on the *imago dei* threatening death to the human spirit. Finally, of course there is salvation: the news of a gracious God who has

not left men and women in the prison of their sin but in Christ
has freed them to 'return'.

It is incontrovertible too that in the moral teaching of Jesus
the love-commandment is primary: all the Law and the
Prophets are summarised in it. In addition, in the teaching and
personal example of Jesus there is abundant illustration of the
quality of the love which is called for. It is in the first place a
matter of the 'heart' (a Hebrew metaphor for the core of the
personality – and, it may be remembered, for conscience), but
it is expressed in action which is provident and caring. It is
universal in its scope: the disciple is asked to love even the
enemy. It is compassionate and forgiving and persists even in
the face of rejection. It is radical and boundlessly generous. It is
like God's love; indeed it *is* God's love, for we are capable of it
only because God first loved us.[5]

It can perhaps be said that a love thus characterised exceeds
the 'merely rational', if rational in this context bespeaks
something which may be concluded as a result of reason's
reflection on human nature. It also makes demands which
appear to transcend what might 'reasonably' be expected: one
of its distinctive features for example is an unlimited readiness
to forgive even those who have done us great wrong. *Agape*, to
use the New Testament's word for this kind of loving, is more
than urbanity.

It may be said also, on the evidence of the biblical material,
that the translation of this love into action displays some
characteristic emphases. There is the readiness to forgive just
mentioned, and a special concern for the widow and the
orphan – Hebrew metaphors for the specially needy. There is
the message of the parable that unless the grain of wheat dies
it does not bring forth fruit. There is the hope that God's reign
will one day be fully established, that a time will come when
God will be all in all.

It will no doubt be noticed, however, that all of these
features – unlimited readiness to forgive, a preoccupation with

justice, a bias toward the specially vulnerable, a willingness to take up one's cross, hope in a resurrection – are in the first place matters of quality and emphasis and orientation. They indicate the *character* of the love to which a disciple is called: the readiness to forgive is unlimited, concern with justice is a 'preoccupation', service of the poor is by way of a 'bias', crucifixion for most is metaphorical. These pointers to the way of Christian discipleship do not on their face say anything about the *content* of concrete action.

Not that the Bible lacks concrete precepts: that is, precepts which name acts or attitudes or states of affairs or omissions enjoined or prohibited by *agape*. 'Thou shall not kill', for example, is a plain statement of the kind of action excluded under the new as under the old covenant. 'Love is patient and kind,' says Paul: 'love is not jealous or boastful; it is not arrogant or rude'.[6] 'It has been reported to me by Chloe's people that there is quarrelling among you,' he writes reprovingly to the Corinthians.[7] 'I was hungry and you gave me no food', the King will say to those on his left hand; 'I was thirsty and you gave me no drink, I was a stranger and you did not welcome me, naked and you did not clothe me, sick and in prison and you did not visit me'.[8]

The precepts, however, of the 'second table' of the Decalogue – those which concern our innerworldly relationships – and the concrete norms of the earliest Christian teaching are, as we have seen, found also outside of the biblical books, for they belong also to the currency of other ethical traditions.[9] We could say that they are the kind of imperative which any well-meaning, right-thinking person might recognise. Reverting to an earlier perspective we might say that we do not need revelation or faith to know of them or to see how they could oblige us. And of course, as we have seen, the concrete norms of biblical times must be interpreted with care, for they were forged in the life of a distant time and place.

Even if, therefore, it be agreed (and agreement, as already said, would presuppose a considerable clarification of terms) that there is some revealed content at the core of the Christian moral scheme, we are not relieved from thinking through the practical demands of morality as these disclose themselves in each age. Our path will be illuminated by the great Christian affirmations about the world and about humanity, our thinking shaped by what has been handed on out of generations of experience of life in the Spirit of Christ, our thinking shaped also by our experience of life in the Christian community now. In this as in other dimensions of the human task, however, grace builds on nature, and there is no shortcut to moral wisdom.[10]

Notes

1   Rom 12:2, and see the rest of the chapter.
2   Meeks, *The Moral World of the First Christians*, London, 13.
3   Meeks, op. cit., 97.
4   Vincent MacNamara, *Faith and Ethics*, Dublin, 1985, 55ff.
5   1 Jn 4:10.
6   1 Cor 13:1.
7   1 Cor 1:11.
8   Mt 25:42,43.
9   See also 1 Cor 5, 6, 7; Eph 4,5,6; Phil 2; 1 Tim 2; Col 3,4; 1 Thess 4; 2 Thess 3; Titus 3.
10   Moral theology has offered various ways of looking at the Christian moral life and it is instructive to compare them. See Cosgrave, 'Models of the Christian Moral Life', op. cit., 9 ff., and Harrington, 'Five Ways of Looking at Morality', op. cit., pp. 9-27.

10

Morality and Spirituality

Studies based on Gallup polls have predicted that the largest sales in non-fiction books in the twenty-first century will be in spirituality / religion.[1] This should not surprise anyone who has watched the extraordinary expansion of titles in this general area, as evidenced by the contents of the shelves of bookshops and of best-seller lists during the past decade or more.[2] If the sales of books (or the proliferation of retreat-centres) is anything to go by there is undoubtedly a widespread interest in spirituality now.

Spirituality

The concept of spirituality is notoriously vague, however, the term is used to cover beliefs and practices as diverse as the occult, self-help programmes and traditional Christian or other religious devotions. Difficulties in pinning down its meaning are no less evident than they are in the case of religion. Once again we are dealing with a subject which occupies entire books, yet again we must opt for a working description or definition which will further our purposes here. We shall not be too far wrong if we adopt the conclusion of one author's review of a range of descriptions available in modern Christian writing.

Michael Downey first sets out the chief of these:

> The term 'spirituality' is used by some to describe the
> depth dimension of all human existence. Here the
> emphasis is on spirituality as a constitutive element of
> human nature and experience. Joann Wolski Conn
> speaks of spirituality in terms of the capacity for self-
> transcendence. For Ewert Cousins, spirituality refers to
> 'the inner dimension of the person...[where] ultimate
> reality is experienced'. John Macquarrie understands
> spirituality to be concerned with 'becoming a person in
> the fullest sense'. For Gordon Wakefield, spirituality has
> to do with 'the constituent of human nature which seeks
> relations with the ground or purpose of human
> existence'. Edward Kinnerk envisions spirituality as the
> expression of the dialectic by which one moves from the
> inauthentic to the authentic. Perhaps the most open-
> ended formulation of all comes from Raimundo
> Pannikar who speaks of spirituality as 'one typical way of
> handling the human condition'.[3]

It might be thought that some of these are not conspicuously
precise, but Downey observes that at any rate there are two
strands which appear to be constants: 'First, and most
importantly, there is an awareness that there are levels of reality
not immediately apparent; there is more than meets the eye.
Second, there is a quest for personal integration in the face of
forces of fragmentation and depersonalization'.[4]

An awareness that 'there is more than meets the eye'? Our
age is an age of observation and measurement, experiment and
verification, empiricism and rationality – the ingredients of
what has become known as the scientific method. It is not
necessary to belittle science and its accomplishments in order
to ask whether it is the only way in which we can understand
ourselves and our world (nor have the greatest scientists

claimed this; think, for example, of Einstein). The 'reasons of the heart' of which Pascal spoke also indicate another kind of knowing, that by which we are sometimes seized in face of beauty or goodness or 'the tears of things'.

A quest for integration? We experience ourselves sometimes as 'broken', 'torn', 'disintegrated', in some way at odds with ourselves and with our world, and we seek 'wholeness' or integration or re-integration. Words of St Paul point to one way in which this experience is encountered: 'The good which I want to do, I fail to do; but what I do is the wrong which is against my will'.[5] Or one might think of the manifold pressures of modern life, and the feelings of alienation and disconnection which can hold us in thrall. We want to recapture moments of ecstasy or of peace, or to find ground on which to stand when we are buffeted. We look for ways in which we might be in touch with what does not meet the eye.

These experiences are difficult to describe, and are perhaps best left to the novelist or dramatist or poet, or indeed the musician or other artist. A poem by R.S. Thomas is suggestive.

That Place
I served on a dozen committees;
talked hard, said little, shared the applause
at the end. Picking over
the remains later, we agreed power
was not ours, launched our invective
at others, the anonymous wielders
of such. Life became small, grey,
the smell of interiors. Occasions
on which a clean air entered our nostrils
off swept seas were instances
we sought to recapture. One particular
time after a harsh morning
of rain, the clouds lifted, the wind

fell; there was a resurrection
of nature, and we there to emerge
with it into the anointed
air. I wanted to say to you: 'We
will remember this.' But tenses
were out of place on that green
island, ringed with the rain's
bow, that we had found and would spend
the rest of our lives looking for.[6]

Morality

But what does all this have to do with morality, with the art of
right relationship with each other and with our world? We have
already seen that the discernment involved in moral decision-
making, or at any rate in moral decision-making of any
complexity, presupposes a meditative or reflective mode. We
don't reach a conclusion as by deduction from some premise,
but rather by 'seeing into' the realities of the situation in which
we have to make our choice. Even for someone who is not
religious, major moral decision making is accomplished in
something like a state of prayer, and it is unlikely that we shall
achieve such a state easily or surely unless we have disposed
ourselves by prior practice.

There is, however, a deeper level at which what Downey
speaks of connects with the moral life. For, as we have also
already seen, how we choose to relate to each other will
depend upon what we make of each other, and what we make
of each other is a matter of vision, of how we 'see' each other
and the world which we inhabit. We may see each other in
different ways – as gift or as threat, as meriting unconditional
regard or as instrument of pleasure or profit, as an 'It' rather
than as a 'Thou', in Martin Buber's terminology.[7] We may see
our world as something to be controlled, manipulated,
exploited for what we conceive to be our benefit, regardless of
the cost to the environment or to non-human inhabitants of

the planet. Or we may see each other and our world as somehow 'sacred'.

Again we meet a word about which we have to be careful. Sacred is by its provenance a religious word; dictionaries commonly render it as consecrated or dedicated to God. But people who are not religious or theist also sometimes speak of a sacredness – of life, of places, of the earth – by which they mean capable of engendering awe, and calling for reverence and respect. So it is that in seeking to relate rightly to the other or to our habitat the first movement of the spirit is a recognition of their value, a value which does not depend on their utility or productivity, still less on their usefulness to ourselves, but which is intrinsic.

A question which then arises is the question how we name the sacred, and it is here that philosophical or religious conviction enters in. It is possible to have an experience such as is here described and to construe it in secular terms; but for many people any adequate interpretation will involve reference to God. The religions commonly point to the grounds of sacredness. The Hebrew Bible, for example, speaks of our being made in the image of God, and the New Testament says that we are temples of the living God,[8] a little less than the angels yet crowned with glory and honour,[9] members of Christ's body.[10] No doubt it is possible simply to reverence life in secular terms; but to be able to see life as God-given, the earth and all that is on it as the work of God's hands, and the human person as daughter or son of God in Christ is to have a powerful ground of reverence and awe.

How we name the sacred, then, or, using Downey's terminology, how we try to name what is 'more than meets the eye', is a matter of our vision or view of life, our *Weltanschauung*, and for many this is religious. Downey, however, speaks also of a quest for integration, and this is characteristically attempted through spiritual disciplines or practices. What is sacred also calls to be 'celebrated', honoured;

and what is sacred can inspire gratitude. All cultures have their rituals by which they celebrate the rising of the sun and its setting, the changing seasons of the year, sowing-time and harvest-time, new life and death. Again one needs to acknowledge that there are secular 'feast days' – there were pagan ones before the Christian, and Christians have adapted some to Christian ends – but again one must remark the way in which so many cultures celebrate life's events with religious rites.

Of course there is as it were a prior need to be 'attuned' to what is more than meets the eye. And so there is a need for 'quiet time', time when we withdraw from immersion in the quotidian and the mundane, time to 'retreat'. The great spiritual traditions are at one in enjoining the setting aside of time during which attempts are made to get in touch with what is more than meets the eye. Which is another way of saying that the religions make time for meditation and contemplation – for 'prayer', however differently this may be conceived as between the different traditions.

As regards the relationship between morality and spirituality, therefore, one might say that morality calls for spirituality or reaches toward it. As we engage in relating with our fellows, as the secrets of the earth (which is our home) disclose themselves, a first reaction must be one of awe, and awe begets reverence and respect. And we shall need to experience this again –

> Occasions
> on which a clean air entered our nostrils
> off swept seas were instances
> we sought to recapture.

Such recapturing is not achieved unless we are attuned, and we shall not be attuned unless we practise staying in touch.

Christian spirituality

The description of spirituality offered by Michael Downey is applicable across the religious and other spiritual traditions, and it has the merit of providing a basis for conversation between them. This is an important and potentially enriching possibility; one thinks of the engagement of the Trappist and Benedictine monks Thomas Merton and Bede Griffiths with Eastern traditions, or the work of the Jesuit William Johnson, and the ongoing dialogue between the Dalai Lama or Thich Nhat Hanh and various Christian spiritual leaders. Some such account provides also for the important possibility of conversation between religious and secular approaches.

In these respects the description resembles that exemplified in our own description of morality. But, as with morality, this approach is not a warrant for any bland reduction of the traditions to some kind of common denominator. There is much that is similar or common, but spiritualities differ too, sometimes in important ways. There is a specificity about Christian (or Jewish or Islamic or Hindu or Buddhist) morality which is irreducible, an identity whereby the Christian's prayer is Christian and not any other. This is what Philip Sheldrake has in mind when he writes:

> The way we understand the concept of 'spirituality' is ultimately dependent on quite specific religious perspectives. In Christian terms, 'spirituality' concerns how people subjectively appropriate traditional beliefs about God, the human person, creation, and their interrelationship, and then express these in worship, basic values and lifestyle. Thus, spirituality is the whole of human life viewed in terms of a conscious relationship with God, in Jesus Christ, through the indwelling of the Spirit and within the community of believers.[11]

What shapes a Christian spirituality, therefore, is the Christian 'story', the lineaments of which we have seen in an earlier chapter – the story of a God who is involved in the creation, who *loves* the creation and wills its rescue from bondage to decay,[12] who is imaged in men and women and wills their liberation from the shackles of sin, who has seen to the accomplishment of this in the personal history of Jesus the Christ, who in Christ invites to repentance and new life. Or, again as we have earlier seen, one might envisage the framework in terms of the great doctrinal affirmations of creation, sin, incarnation, redemption and resurrection. It is in such faith-statements that the touchstones of a Christian spirituality are to be found, as it is in them that the specific truth-claims of Christianity are expressed.

Space again constrains so that there can be no question of a comprehensive account, but it may be useful to point to salient features of mainline Christian spirituality. First, it is not to be thought of as just a matter of prayer or liturgical practice, as though these were activities separate from 'life'. The Eucharist is at the centre of worship; but the Eucharist sends the communicant back into the world, so to say, in order to live the life which he or she has professed at the altar. There is 'communion', with God in sacrament, and with each other as brothers and sisters around the altar; but the worshipper who affirms communion is by that fact undertaking to act as sister or brother.

Second, and otherwise than has sometimes been portrayed in the past, spirituality is not an elite preoccupation but a mode of being in the world to which all are called. The awareness which is its mark, the reverence which it begets, the 'attunement' which it makes possible – these are not just for the monk and the nun but for each Christian.[13] Nor does it mean disregard for the secular, for the goods and beauties of the earth, the achievements of the human mind at its finest. And it calls for a care for the earth and all that is on it; a concern for all that is now signified by the term ecology is an imperative of the Christian way.[14]

In the course of this book we have distinguished first between religion and morality, then between morality and spirituality, and now between spirituality and religion; and we have done this because they are separable aspects of experience, and because there are people who live happily with a 'religionless' morality and spirituality. But of course there is some artificiality in the distinctions as far as a religious believer is concerned – and even, *mutatis mutandis*, in the case of someone who is not a believer. For we do not see the other, or our world, by way of a 'pure' reason; our way of seeing and of thinking are already shaped by what I have been calling our vision of life.

Yet it remains true that the moral claim, the moral point of view, is not dependent on religious faith, as we have so often seen; it is a demand of our humanness or rationality; in the words of MacNamara again, 'the very existence of others itself makes a claim on us'.[15] And being moral, for the Christian as for anyone else, is essentially recognising this claim. 'But Christians do not split themselves into religious and moral compartments. Their religious story informs, enriches and shapes this basic perception. It suggests a fuller understanding of the indefeasible value of the other.... And, like every primordial story, it necessarily has a viewpoint on how the content – the main lines – of response to the other is to be filled in'.[16] The religious and the moral and the spiritual mesh, and the truth-claims of the Christian faith, as those of any vision of life, must in the end be confronted.

Notes

1   Michael Downey, *Understanding Christian Spirituality*, Mahwah NJ, 1997, 6. 'The projection is that there will be an 82 percent growth in these books between 1987 and 2010.'

2   From September 1998, for almost two years, a book called *Anam Cara* was in or near top place in the Irish non-fiction best-seller list. *Anam Cara* is by John O'Donohue, and is an exploration of the spiritual using Christian and non-Christian sources. For fifteen months unbroken it was first on the list, displaced to second very briefly by a biography of Mary Robinson, and later by a book by Sister Stanislaus Kennedy (itself a book on spirituality) recovering first place again and succeeded by a second book by O'Donohue called *Eternal Echoes*.

3   Downey, op. cit., 14. Vincent MacNamara's *New Life for Old*, Dublin, 2004, is an invaluable resource as regards the relationships between morality, spirituality and religious faith.

4   Ibid.

5   Rom 7:19.

6   'That Place', from R.S. Thomas, *Later Poems '72–'82* (London: Macmillan, 1983), p.53.

7   Martin Buber, *I and Thou*, Edinburgh and New York, 1958.

8   2 Cor 6:16

9   Heb 2:7 .

10   Rom 12:5.

11   Philip Sheldrake, *Spirituality and Theology*, London, 1998, 34, 35.

12   Rom 8:21.

13   So the Second Vatican Council: 'The Lord Jesus, divine teacher and model of all perfection, preached holiness of life (of which he is the author and maker) to each and every one of his disciples without distinction . . . It is therefore quite clear that all Christians in any state or walk of life are called to the fullness of Christian life and to the perfection of love, and by this holiness a more human manner of life is fostered also in earthly society'. (*Lumen Gentium*, par 40)

14   Mark O'Keefe has summarised recent trends in Catholic writing on spirituality: 'sustained attention to a more holistic understanding of spirituality; the effort to undercut any form of dualism which would excessively separate mundane life and activity from some "other-worldly" spiritual realm; the more interdisciplinary approach of spirituality; the conviction that prayer and action are two dimensions of the human person which must be held

together; a greater awareness of the ecological impact of spiritualities; and the recognition of the need to retrieve the insights of the past': *Becoming Good, Becoming Holy*, New York/Mahwah, 1995, 20.

15   Vincent MacNamara, 'The Distinctiveness of Christian Morality', in Bernard Hoose, *Ethics: an Introduction*, 153.

16   Ibid.

11

Morality and Law

Our lives are shaped by both morality and law, and sometimes we may confuse the one with the other. Of course morality itself is often called the moral law, but the law now in question is that made by those who have governance of a society – 'positive' law, as it is sometimes called, from a Latin word which means to lay down. This law is there because it was enacted by a lawmaker in some sense of that expression, or perhaps because it grew out of custom. In modern experience it is usually written, and its precepts are to be found in constitutions, charters and statute-books and, in some systems, in the decisions of judges.

Morality and law resemble each other: each has to do with the regulation of behaviour, each deals in rules which enjoin or forbid certain acts or omissions or states of affairs. Morality requires that we respect human life, the law that we drive on a particular side of the road. It is morally wrong to drive in a way that endangers life; it is illegal to exceed the speed limit. In some matters, the scopes of law and morality overlap: both forbid murder, perjury, rape and theft, for example. They intersect in other ways too, for law needs the support of morality, and aspects of morality may be expressed in law; and morality normally requires that we obey the law.

The two spheres differ also, however, and the differences are profoundly important. For one thing – a point which we have glimpsed already – they differ in their origins: one has its roots in reasoned reflection on our nature, the other in a lawmaker's *fiat*. Relatedly, the source of obligation of each is different: for morality, reason's understanding of the exigencies of human flourishing; for law, the will of the ruler or of whomever is the bearer of authority in the *polis*.

Another difference is that morality pays attention to internal factors such as disposition or attitude or intention, whereas a good deal of law does not. From the law's point of view it doesn't matter with what degree of resentment I pay my taxes: if I pay them I comply with the law. From a moral point of view, however, resentment may mar what is ostensibly correct, as when I do a good deed with bad grace. Similarly, if I wrong someone inadvertently I cannot be blamed morally, since I didn't mean to do so, but, if inadvertently I exceed the speed limit or fail to pay my TV licence, I can only hope for the indulgence of Garda or judge; I stand liable to punishment, for I have broken, unquestionably, the law. An incidental implication is that compliance with the law is no guarantee of moral worth; and indeed morality may require that we disobey a law, a proposition which we must look at more closely later.

Four questions
H.L.A. Hart has listed the main questions which may be put about the relationships between morality and law. The first is whether the development of law has been influenced by morality (and vice versa); the second, whether some reference to morality must enter into an adequate definition of law. A third asks whether the law is open to moral criticism, and the fourth is whether it is the business of the law to enforce morality – more exactly, to make immorality a crime.[1] The second and third questions have often been debated by moralists and legal philosophers, and we shall shortly meet a

practical illustration of their significance. The fourth question
has long been associated with the name of John Stuart Mill,
though nowadays it is more likely to evoke the names of Devlin
and Hart and the debate engendered by their exchanges.

The first question is briefly dealt with: it seems clear that the
development of law is influenced by morality, even if morality
is not always the sole influence. An example is that of
legislation aimed at ending discrimination on the basis of race
or gender; for the impulse toward this sort of legislation comes
from the moral insight that people should be treated equally.
Similarly, legislation concerning conditions in the workplace is
founded on such considerations as the dignity of the person,
the right to fair remuneration, and the need to preclude
exploitation – all of which are issues of morality.

That law may influence the development of morality seems
equally clear. Legislation concerning drink driving was greeted
with reluctance by many drivers, and it may be complied with
only for fear of punishment, so that the moral value of
compliance in an individual case is slight if it exists at all. Yet
there are many drivers who, though they complied at first
reluctantly, do so now more freely, because they have come to
recognise that this law concerns the protection of life and the
elimination of a threat to life and bodily integrity. Free choice
of an action which is perceived to be for good is of course what
we mean by moral choice.[2]

Law and moral obligation

The second and third questions are related: whether a reference
to morality must enter into an adequate definition of law, and
whether the law is open to moral criticism; and they bear directly
upon the question of whether there is a moral obligation to obey
the law. For if it is necessary for the validity of a law that it not
be immoral, immorality is a basis for disobedience.

Now normally we are obliged to keep the law of the land,
and it is morally wrong to do what is illegal. For laws are laid

down in aid of community welfare, and compliance with them is usually a precondition of human flourishing. But a law may be immoral, as when it discriminates unfairly on the basis of race or religion or sex, or a law might enjoin immorality, as in Hitler's Germany in relation to Jews. From a moral standpoint it will not do to seek to justify oneself by saying 'I obeyed the law', or to defend a wrong done under the law by saying 'I was only obeying orders'. For all that we are normally obliged to keep the law there may be times when we are obliged to disobey.

This last theme is as old as Antigone, yet as fresh in the memory as the Nürnberg trials after the Second World War. Antigone buried her brother Polyneices, defying an order made by Creon, king of Thebes, who had forbidden him honourable burial. In Sophocles' play she defends herself by appeal to a higher law, and Seamus Heaney's rendering captures the drama and the sense:

> I disobeyed because the law was not
> The law of Zeus nor the law ordained
> By Justice, Justice dwelling deep
> Among the gods of the dead. What they decree
> Is immemorial and binding for us all.
> The proclamation had your force behind it
> But it was a mortal force, and I also a mortal,
> I chose to disregard it. I abide
> By statutes utter and immutable –
> Unwritten, original, god-given laws.[3]

The notion of a higher law to which even rulers are answerable has persisted in Western thinking in the form of some version of the doctrine of a 'Natural Law'. Not, as we saw, that all versions of the doctrine have come to the same thing, and no version has escaped criticism. Yet commentators have seen some such notion at work even in the ostensibly 'positivist' climate of the Nürnberg tribunal for the trial of war crimes. 'An order is an order', the accused officials and officers pleaded, meaning that they were obliged to do what was commanded by superiors, and thus were justified in acting as they did. But the plea did not succeed, and A.P. d'Entrèves has written: 'The rejection of the defence of superior orders... is nothing less than the old doctrine that the validity of laws does not depend on their "positiveness", and that it is the duty of the individual to pass judgment on laws before he obeys them'.[4]

The enforcement of morals

Hart's fourth question, whether it is the business of the law to enforce morality 'as such', that is, to proscribe immorality just because it is immoral, was the subject of a debate between himself and Sir Patrick (later Lord) Devlin, following publication of the latter's Maccabean lecture entitled 'Morals and the Criminal Law'. It is worth paying attention to some of the detail of that debate, for this fourth question is one with which we have become familiar; and when one looks at the arguments made by each of the protagonists, it can be seen that they are echoed in our own public debates. The question has become complicated by reason of what is usually called the pluralism of moral belief and practice which is a feature of life today, but we can conveniently leave this aspect of the question until the next chapter.

Devlin's lecture was a critique of the report of a committee which, under the chairmanship of Lord Wolfenden, had been charged with the task of making proposals for the reform of the law on prostitution and on homosexual activity. Wolfenden's committee had sought a principle which would allow it to address both sets of concerns in a consistent way, and they found it in a version of a principle first enunciated by John Stuart Mill.

In *On Liberty*, Mill wrote that the only purpose for which the criminal law can rightfully be used is to prevent harm to others.[5] The version espoused by the committee is that the function of the criminal law is 'to preserve public order and decency, to protect the citizen from what is offensive or injurious, and to provide sufficient safeguards against exploitation and corruption of others, particularly the young, weak in body and mind, inexperienced, or in a state of special physical, official or economic dependence'[6]. Devlin interpreted this to mean that 'no act of immorality should be made a criminal offence unless it is accompanied by some other feature such as indecency, corruption or exploitation',[7] or if it injures someone's person or property. Features such as these are what, according to Wolfenden, bring immorality into the public domain. And only when there is this public dimension is it permissible for the law to take an interest.

Devlin rejected the Wolfenden view, and his position may be put summarily as follows. People who form a civil society do so on the basis of certain shared ideas, including ideas about right and wrong. A society's existence is threatened if members deviate from the morality so shared, and it is as entitled to protect itself from moral subversion as from political. It is for society to say how much deviance it will tolerate, and it is entitled to use the criminal law to enforce its morality when deviance exceeds toleration's bounds. A legislator will know when this point has been reached by reference to the standard of the reasonable man [sic], 'the man on the Clapham omnibus'.[8]

On this view there is no private immorality in the sense envisaged by the Wolfenden committee. The most private of acts has a social resonance, however indirectly produced: *any* immorality is of its nature capable of threatening a society's existence. In theory therefore there is no immoral act that might not be forbidden by law. But in practice a line must be drawn, for the individual 'cannot be expected to surrender to the judgement of society the whole conduct of his life'. Therefore, in deciding what to proscribe, a lawmaker may be helped by some general principles.

Private and public morality

Before reviewing these it might be useful to look more closely at a key question upon which Devlin and Hart were at odds: whether there is a 'private morality' which is, as Wolfenden put it, not the law's business. The expression 'private morality' was to prove troublesome, and it may be as well at this point to be clear at least about what it does *not* mean. For a start it doesn't make sense to think of it as referring to the morality of acts done in private; most murders are done in private, and privacy is virtually essential to the thief; and it would be ludicrous to suggest that the law should never intervene when a man beats his wife or children at home.

Nor is it helpful to think of the term 'private morality' as referring to what is a matter of private (in the sense of personal) moral judgement. For the question whether something is properly left to the individual's conscience or whether, rather, it is a claim of the moral order, is usually only the starting-point of a debate. So, for example, the claim that women have a moral right to choose abortion comes up against the claim that the unborn have a moral right to life from conception. The first claim says that it is a matter for the personal conscience of a woman whether to have an abortion or not, the second – in a familiar version – maintains that the moral order precludes the directly intended taking of any innocent life. The argument cannot be settled by *asserting* the one right or the other, and there remains for the legislator the question whether or how either of these beliefs is to be 'enforced'.

The Devlin-Hart debate

And so we return to the question at the centre of the debate between Devlin and Hart: is there a 'public morality' which it is the law's business to enforce? Devlin, we saw, contended that there is, and that it is discerned by reference to the standard of the 'reasonable man'; and he also offered some principles that might guide the legislator in deciding which items of this public morality ought to be enforced by law.

The first of these principles – Devlin calls them 'elastic' - is that there should be the maximum freedom consistent with the integrity of society. The law should not attempt to enforce all of a society's moral code, but only those items without the observance of which society would disintegrate. Second, says Devlin, the law should move slowly, for the limits of society's tolerance are apt to shift from time to time. Third, as far as possible privacy should be respected, he sees a value in allowing people what would nowadays be called their personal space. Finally, the fourth principle is that the law is concerned with minimum and not maximum standards of behaviour, and it should not try to do too much.

Lord Devlin's thesis was challenged by H.L.A Hart, whose position was essentially that of Mill and the Wolfenden committee. The detail of their exchanges (for the debate did not end with Hart's rejoinder to the Maccabean lecture) is beyond the scope of a short chapter, but one should notice Hart's starting-point, for it sets the tone of his contribution as a whole. It is the contention that the question whether morals should be enforced *is itself a moral question*: enforcement involves the curtailment of freedom, and the curtailment of freedom requires moral justification.

In support of this Hart points out that legal enforcement has two aspects. The first is that it involves the punishment of offenders, and this is typically done by depriving them of freedom of movement or of property or of association with family or friends, or the infliction of physical pain or even death. All of these, however, are normally regarded as evil, and normally their infliction is considered wrong. If, therefore, it is to escape moral censure, their infliction requires special justification. The second aspect of enforcement is no less pertinent to the need for justification: it is that law restricts freedom also in coercing conformity through threat of punishment. One's freedom is just as surely, even if differently, inhibited when one refrains from some act for fear of being put in jail as it is when one is jailed for doing the forbidden deed.

For all that there are differences between the two views, they are not without common ground. Both envisage the main issue as one of reconciling personal freedom and the public interest, in some sense of that expression. Each requires advertence to a social dimension in human conduct, and to a public interest in preventing social harm; and each is prepared to recognise a role for law in that process. Indeed one commentator has said that 'both are recognizably liberal'[9], meaning no doubt that each puts a premium on freedom.

In Hart's case this is clear even in the way he frames the main question, but it is intimated also in Devlin's assertion that 'the individual has a *locus standi* too; he cannot be expected to surrender to the judgement of society the whole conduct of his life'.[10] This insight is made concrete in the 'elastic principles' to which Devlin would have the legislator advert, and especially in the requirements that there should be toleration of maximum freedom consistent with the integrity of society, and that privacy must as far as possible be respected.

It may be, as is sometimes suggested, that the principal difference between them is one of emphasis; but the difference in emphasis is critical. Devlin's overriding interest is in the 'integrity of society', and in that sense he is 'conservative'. Hart's concern, first and last, is with the protection of individual freedom. Devlin's way of looking at the issues will probably recommend itself to someone whose instinct is to preserve societal values, Hart's will be the more congenial for someone who is inclined to a more 'liberal' political view.

Of course, strictly speaking the term 'enforcement of morals' is a misnomer. For the law can at best ensure only external compliance, whereas to be moral it is not enough to behave in a way which is merely externally correct.[11] Hence it seems better to say that what the law enforces is a moral *code*, or at least that part of a code which commands or prohibits observable conduct; that it cannot enforce morality 'as such'. Indeed if someone refrains from misconduct wholly out of fear of punishment it is hardly correct to speak of morality at all.

This provides a clue, as James Mackey has suggested, to the truth that emerges from the Devlin-Hart debate, and it shows that each was partly right. 'Law does, and must always, make its business what would be morally right for people to do or to refrain from doing. That is always true of law, in any form of human society which proposes itself to be essential to human living... This is the part of the truth that Devlin protected so well on his side of the debate.'[12] But it is the merit of Hart's contribution that 'he has pointed unerringly to the quite literally demoralising tendency of the apparatus of extraneous punishment and of its ever-present threat'.[13]

To be sure, as we have seen, law has an educational function; but the notion of the law as pedagogue must be viewed with caution. Law does reflect a community's values, and there is a 'rhetoric of law'[14] which signals something of the importance which a society attaches to the values which its members profess to hold. Furthermore, modern practice as regards, for example, equality or health legislation, or such legislation as there is concerning the environment, acknowledges a right and responsibility on the part of government to promote behaviour called for by a moral responsibility. We need not, however, expect law by itself to make people good, and there is no substitute for moral education.

Notes

1   *Law, Liberty and Morality*, Oxford, 1968, 1ff.
2   In the medieval tradition Aquinas had a high idea of law's place: he included it among the ways in which God 'educates' people in goodness. His account of how this happens is nuanced, and his expectations of law were modest. Yet he is clear that it has a role.

'From becoming accustomed to shun what is evil and discharge what is good on account of threat of punishment a man sometimes comes to continue on that course from his own taste and choice. Hence law even as punitive brings men to good.' *Summa Theologiae*, 1a2ae, 92, art 2 ad 4, Blackfriars edn, London, 1966, vol. 28, 28. We should no doubt in any case acknowledge that human motivation is rarely pure.

3   *The Burial at Thebes: Sophocles' Antigone*, tr. Seamus Heaney, London, 2004. A more conventional translation is in *Theban Plays*, tr. E.F. Watling, Harmondsworth, 1967, 138.

4   At Nürnberg, d'Entrèves notes, 'the provisions for the... Tribunal were based, or purported to be based, on existing or "positive" international law'. Nevertheless d'Entrèves believes, 'the boundaries of legal positivism were overstepped... the moment it was stated that the trials were "a question of justice"', *Natural Law*, 106. Positivism is a theory of law which holds that law is simply what is commanded by the legislator, and that its validity depends on strictly legal (and not moral) criteria.

5   Ed. G. Himmelfarb, Harmondsworth, 1974, 68.

6   Patrick Devlin, *The Enforcement of Morals*, Oxford, 1965, 2

7   op. cit., 3.

8   Lawyers' jargon for the 'ordinary' person.

9   Basil Mitchell, *Law, Morality and Religion in a Secular Society*, Oxford, 1967, 18.

10   Devlin, *The Enforcement of Morals*, 15.

11   In this connection it is interesting to read what Aquinas has to say about the law's role in regard to virtue: *Summa Theologiae* I-II, q. 96, art. 4. Notice also his realism concerning the use of the law in restraining vice: I-II, q. 96, art.3; and see note 2 above.

12   James P. Mackey, *Power and Christian Ethics*, Cambridge 1994, 52.

13   Ibid.

14   The term is Mary Ann Glendon's, and it is explored in her *Abortion and Divorce in Western Law*, Harvard, 1987.

12

Pluralism and the Common Good

It was observed in the preceding chapter that the question of the enforcement of morals, as it is called, is complicated nowadays by a pluralism of moral as well as religious belief and practice in Ireland as in other western societies. For if it is the case that the law reflects a people's values, and that some laws may be said to enforce them, whose values should a legal system reflect or enforce? The values of the majority religious (or other) moral tradition? What then of minorities in the community: are they to be coerced into following patterns of behaviour which are contrary to conscience, or prevented from acting according to their consciences, simply because the majority subscribes to a different world-view?

Pluralism need mean no more than that there is a factual diversity of belief and practice in religious and moral matters in the world at large or within a particular community. In this sense there has always been a pluralism in morals, certainly in the world at large and even in regions and countries. If we are more aware of such diversity the reason is doubtless in modern possibilities for communication; one need only allude to the 'revolution' in communications technology and the relative facility with which a modern may travel the world.

Of course, this awareness breeds questions for value systems if only by showing the viability – not to mention the rival attractions – of alternatives. In modern experience this combines with the democratic instinct so as to create a demand for the legitimation within communities of political or moral viewpoints hitherto looked on as deviant. If formerly the practical implementation of such a viewpoint was precluded by the law, the demand for its recognition now quite naturally takes the shape of a call for legal change.

In making the case for any change in the law it is not enough to invoke a vague generalisation about the rights of minorities in a pluralist society. For there are minorities in our societies whose behaviour we shouldn't dream of sanctioning by way of legal toleration: criminals, for example, or subversives in the political order. It must be obvious that the mere fact that a belief is held by a minority, even a notable minority, is not enough to ground a case for change.

This is elementary – though sometimes apparently overlooked – and it is an obvious reason for the opposition of some people to arguments which appeal to pluralism. Another reason is that the appeal is thought to imply the view that one set of moral values is as good as another. It is interesting to recall that a similar apprehension underlay resistance to the principle of what is usually called religious freedom, now a part of the official doctrine of the Catholic Church. But as the *Declaration on Religious Freedom* of the Second Vatican Council makes plain, religious indifferentism is not a necessary premise of the principle of religious freedom. Nor does conviction of the truth of one's own faith preclude an effective respect for the religious beliefs of others.

A starting point – the Declaration on Religious Freedom
One of the reasons why it is difficult to think clearly about these questions is that it is difficult to find a starting-point that has prospect of common acceptance. One can argue, however,

that, for all that it comes from a particular religious tradition, Roman Catholic teaching concerning religious freedom provides a starting-point, and indeed the makings of a framework, for fruitful discussion on the issues at stake. The reason why it has prospect of a more general acceptance is that its basis is a philosophical one, of a kind which resonates with the mind of our times.

The teaching of the Council on religious freedom represented the maturation of ideas whose seedbed was the US experience of Catholicism and whose most eloquent exponent was the American Jesuit John Courtney Murray. As articulated during the nineteenth century the official stance of Roman Catholicism *vis-à-vis* other faiths (or non-faith) was at best one of grudging toleration. 'Error has no rights' was the basic maxim: ideally religious error should be proscribed, though in concrete circumstances it might be granted a provisional toleration for fear of greater evil. The Council's achievement in regard to religious freedom was the replacement of this doctrine with one developed in the thought of Courtney Murray.

The Declaration's starting-point is the modern consciousness of the dignity of the human person, and the growing demand that people 'should exercise fully their own judgment and a responsible freedom in their actions, and should not be subject to the pressure of coercion but be inspired by a sense of duty'.[1] This demand is 'concerned chiefly with ... spiritual values, and especially with what concerns the free practice of religion in society'.[2] Attentive to these 'spiritual aspirations', the Council wishes to search Church tradition 'from which it draws forth new things that are always in harmony with the old'.[3]

The Council then professes its belief that God's truth was revealed in Jesus Christ. It believes moreover that 'this one true religion continues to exist in the Catholic and Apostolic Church', to which the Lord gave the task of spreading it to all;

and all have a duty to seek the truth, and to live by it as they come to know it.[4] It is plain that the Council does not wish to diminish a whit the religious claims of the Catholic Church, or to lend any support to religious indifferentism. There is a revealed truth, it continues to maintain, to be found now in the faith of the Catholic Church, and everyone is bound to seek out the truth as best he or she may. Acknowledgment of a religious pluralism is not meant to suggest that one religion is as good as another. Nevertheless '[t]he Vatican Council declares that the human person has a right to religious freedom'.[5]

A principle

I shall argue later that though the Council's doctrine concerns religious (as distinct from moral) freedom of belief and practice, it affords guidance also as regards morality. First, however, we must see the meaning of the teaching and its basis. In the words of the Council:

> Freedom of this kind means that all should be immune from coercion on the part of individuals, social groups and every human power so that, within due limits, no men or women are forced to act against their convictions nor are any persons to be restrained from acting in accordance with their convictions in religious matters in private or in public, alone or in association with others. The Council further declares that the right to religious freedom is based on the very dignity of the human person as known through the revealed word of God and by reason itself. This right of the human person to religious freedom must be given such recognition in the constitutional order of society as will make it a civil right.[6]

The principle therefore has two aspects: people should not be forced to act against their religious beliefs, nor should they be restrained from acting in their light; and this goes for the public as for the private domain. The qualification 'within due limits' is plainly of the greatest significance and we shall have to return to it shortly.

The basis for the principle is the dignity of the person: 'It is in accordance with their dignity that all human beings, because they are persons, that is beings endowed with reason and free will and therefore bearing personal responsibility, are both impelled by their nature and bound by a moral obligation to seek the truth, especially religious truth'.[7]

Human dignity resides in our being gifted with reason and freedom, and it belongs to our nature that we should look for the truth and live by it. 'But [people] cannot satisfy this obligation in a way that is in keeping with their own nature unless they enjoy both psychological freedom and immunity from external coercion'.[8]

Note that the Council says that the right to religious freedom is founded not in the subjective attitude of the person but in human nature. 'For this reason the right to immunity continues to exist even in those who do not live up to their obligation of seeking the truth and adhering to it.'[9] And again there is a practical corollary: 'The exercise of this right cannot be interfered with as long as the just requirements of public order are observed.'[10]

This is the second mention of a restriction of the exercise of the right to religious freedom: reference to 'the just requirements of public order' may be read as a gloss on the earlier expression 'within due limits'. The concrete significance of the restriction is later indicated, in general and in particular. In general, 'in availing [sic] of any freedom people must respect the principle of personal and social responsibility: in exercising their rights, individuals and social groups are bound by the moral law to have regard for the rights of others, their own duties to others and the common good of all'.[11] In particular, people's freedom is limited by the requirements of peace, justice and public morality, all of which are 'basic to the common good and belong to what is called public order'.[12] After this fairly standard statement of the need to reconcile the enjoyment of rights with the facts of life in society the last word is given to freedom: 'For the rest, the principle of the integrity of freedom in society should continue to be upheld. According to this principle people's freedom should be given the fullest possible recognition and should not be curtailed except when and in so far as is necessary'.[13]

As observed earlier, the Declaration is concerned with *religious* freedom as such, and one needs to argue explicitly in favour of its application to morality. The argument is not, however, complicated. For the principle is based on the dignity of the person and on the character of the search for truth, and these are in essence the same whether one is thinking of religion or of morality. As gifted with reason and choice we live up to our dignity to the extent that we freely seek and live moral truth; and coercion is no more at home in the quest for moral than it is for religious value.

We may, therefore, formulate a principle by analogy. In moral matters people should not be forced to act against their consciences, nor should they be restrained from behaving according to conscience – provided that 'the just requirements of public order' are observed. In morality as in religion there should be freedom of belief and action, in public and in private, for individuals and for groups, subject only to the requirements of peace, justice and public morality. These are the 'due limits' of an earlier paragraph, and in Catholic theology they are the touchstones of the 'common good'.

The common good

The expression common good is a familiar one in Catholic social teaching since the time of Pope Leo XIII in the second half of the nineteenth century, but its roots are in ancient Greek and Roman thought, and it is used in Christian theology from at least the time of St Augustine. Aquinas regarded it as one of the defining features of law, which he described as a rational ordinance 'for the common good' made by those who have care of the community and promulgated.[14] Our purposes do not require the detail which a full account would call for, and we can work with a description offered elsewhere by the Council and reproduced with minor modifications in the *Declaration*.[15]

The common good, according to the Constitution on the Church in the Modern World is 'the sum total of social conditions which enable people, either as groups or as individuals, to reach their fulfilment more fully and more easily'.[16] Even from this description it is possible to see that it is not something as it were set over against individual good. Indeed John Finnis has remarked that the modern 'manifesto' conception of human rights 'is a way of sketching *the outlines of the common good*, the various aspects of individual well-being in community'[17]. Thus personal freedom is itself a part of the common good; and care of the common good includes the promotion of all human rights, personal and social.[18]

This is an important point, because the term is often used in public debate as though it meant something wholly separate from the freedom of individuals. Some speak of it as though it were the good of the majority, or even of the State, so that the recognition of a minority or personal freedom is subject to its according with the beliefs of the majority or with some objective of the State. Those who argue in this fashion appear untroubled by the realisation that on the logic of their position some of their own freedoms might be abridged in a society in which the majority is of a different religious or moral (or political) persuasion; nor do they seem to recognise that theirs is the logic of totalitarianism or what Jacques Maritain called state despotism.

There is more to the common good than personal freedom and individual rights, however, as we can see when we recall that in life in society the freedoms of the members require to be harmonised so that *each* person can flourish in the optimum measure. And this means, first, retrieval of a sense of community, and of solidarity in community, qualities not yet entirely lost in today's Ireland but which need attention and sustenance as a matter of urgency.

In this process government and law have a role, characterised in Catholic social teaching (following continental civil code use[19]) as the preservation of a 'public order', but more amply described as the promotion of a common good. It is easy to see why this is said to include public peace and justice; but what are we to make of the concept of 'public morality'? Here of course we rejoin the Devlin-Hart debate and the discussion which this has generated, and we are soon led to a major theme in modern political philosophy. I suggested earlier that each of us may see our own sympathies mirrored in the positions of the protagonists in the debate between Devlin and Hart, and by the same token we see the makings of a critique of whichever of the two views attracts. Perhaps, however, the most important thing about that debate now is that it forces us onward to think about the question, what kind of society do we want and how are we to achieve it?

Notes

1   Par.1, Fl 551.
2   Ibid.
3   Ibid.
4   Ibid.
5   Par.2, Fl 552.
6   Fl 552, 553.
7   Fl 553.
8   Ibid.
9   Ibid.
10   Ibid.
11   Par.7, Fl 558.
12   Ibid.

13   Ibid.

14   *Summa Theologiae* 1a 2ae, 90, 2. Bl 28. For Aquinas the common
     good was a complex concept whose political application was only
     one aspect: see Bl 28, Appendix 4, 172-4.

15   A classic text is still Jacques Maritain, *The Person and the Common
     Good,* New York, 1947; see also his *The Rights of Man,* London,
     1944. For further study, two indispensable books are David
     Hollenbach SJ, *The Common Good and Christian Ethics,* Cambridge,
     2002, and Patrick Riordan SJ, *A Politics of the Common Good,* Dublin,
     1996; each of these repays careful study.

16   *Gaudium et Spes* 26, Fl 191. Cp. the *Declaration*: 'The common good
     of society consists in the sum total of those conditions of social life
     which enable people to achieve a fuller measure of perfection with
     greater ease' – par.6, Fl 556. These descriptions echo the encyclical
     Mater et Magistra of Pope John XXIII.

17   John Finnis, *Natural Law and Natural Rights,* Oxford, 1980, 214.

18   Note also *Gaudium et Spes,* par. 26: 'Every group must take into
     account the legitimate rights and aspirations of every other group,
     and even those of the human family as a whole'.

19   In common law systems, including that of Ireland, the term public
     order has the narrower sense of absence of disorder; see Finnis op.
     cit.

Select Bibliography

A. Moral Theology Textbooks

Useful introductory texts include:

Bretzke, James T., *A Morally Complex World: Engaging Contemporary Moral Theology*, Collegeville, 2004

Gascoigne, Robert, *Freedom and Purpose*, New York/Mahwah, 2004

Gula, Richard M., *Reason Informed by Faith*, New York/Mahwah, 1989

Hoose, Bernard (ed.), *Christian Ethics: an Introduction*, London, 1998

Kelly, Kevin T., *New Directions in Moral Theology*, London/New York, 1992

MacNamara, Vincent, *The Truth in Love*, Dublin, 1988 (Also published as *Love, Law and the Christian Life*, Delaware, 1988)

Miller, Mark, *Making Moral Choices: an Introduction*, Mystic, Ct, 1995

Spohn, William C., *Go and Do Likewise*, New York, 2000

See also the series entitled *What Are They Saying?*, published by Paulist Press, New York/Mahwah, especially the volumes by William Spohn, *What Are They Saying About Scripture and Ethics?*, and Richard Gula, *What Are They Saying About Moral Norms?*. A

non-technical overview of some of the main themes is in Patrick
Hannon, *Knowing Right from Wrong?* (Dublin: Veritas, 1995).

An introductory text incorporating Christian ecumenical
perspectives is *The Cambridge Companion to Christian Ethics*, ed.
Robin Gill, Cambridge, 2001.

A scholarly work, including historical material, is S.
Pinckaers, *The Sources of Christian Ethics,* tr. M.N. Noble,
Washington, 1995. See also J. Mahoney, *The Makings of Moral
Theology*, Oxford, 1989.

B. Moral Philosophy

*There are numerous helpful introductions to moral philosophy, among
which are:*

Almond, Brenda, *Exploring Ethics: a Traveller's Tale*, Malden,
    Mass., 1998
Benn, Piers, *Ethics*, London, 1998
Bowie, Robert, *Ethical Studies* (2nd edn), Cheltenham, 2004
Frankena, William, *Ethics* (2nd edn), Englewood Cliffs, NJ,
    1973*
Gensler, Harry J., *Ethics: a Contemporary Introduction*,
    London/New York, 1998
Gensler, Harry J. et al (eds), *Ethics: Contemporary Readings,* New
    York/London, 2004
Lovibond, Sabina, *Ethical Formation*, Cambridge
    Mass./London, 2002
McGrath, Elizabeth, *The Art of Ethics: a Psychology of Ethical
    Beliefs*, Chicago, 1994
McNaughton, David, *Moral Vision: an Introduction to Ethics*,
    Oxford, 1988
Pojman, Louis, *Ethics: Discovering Right and Wrong* (4th edn),
    Belmont CA, 2002
Raphael, David D., *Moral Philosophy*, Oxford, 1994*
Rist, John, *Real Ethics: Reconsidering the Foundations of Morality,*
    Cambridge, 2002

Thompson, Mel, *Ethical Theory*, London, 1999
Williams, Bernard, *Morality: an Introduction to Ethics*, Harmondsworth, 1972*

* Each of these is a minor 'classic', extremely useful, though in terms of recent writing not so up to date as others on the list.

C. Ethics and World Religions

Philip Barnes' *World Religions* in the present series is a fine general introduction to the theology of the world religions.

Each of the following (in the OUP *Very Short Introduction* series) provides a good general introduction and includes bibliography.
Keown, Damien, *Buddhism*, Oxford, 2000
Knott, Kim, *Hinduism*, Oxford, 1998
Ruthven, Malise, *Islam*, Oxford, 2000
Solomon, Norman, *Judaism*, Oxford, 1996

A book in this series on Buddhist ethics by Damien Keown and one on Christianity by Linda Woodhead are forthcoming; and see the list of titles included in each volume for others which may be helpful in connection with the course.

A well-known and recommended account of Islam is Jacques Jomier's *How to Understand Islam*, 1989.

D. Readings

The fourteen volumes in the series entitled *Readings in Moral Theology*, edited by Charles E. Curran and Richard A. McCormick, published by Paulist Press, are indispensable accompaniments to the further study of Catholic moral theology. They contain seminal articles in each major area. In connection with the present text, see especially volumes one (moral norms), two (distinctiveness of Christian ethics), three (magisterium and morality), four (scripture and moral theology), seven (natural law), and fourteen (conscience).

E. Conscience

D'Arcy, Eric, *Conscience and Its Right to Freedom*, London, 1962

Hogan, Linda, *Confronting the Truth: Conscience in the Catholic Tradition*, London, 2001

Hoose, Jayne (ed.), *Conscience in World Religions*, Leominster/Notre Dame, 1999

Nelson, C. Ellis (ed.), *Conscience: Theological and Psychological Perspectives*, New York, 1973

Potts, Timothy, *Conscience in Medieval Philosophy*, Cambridge, 1980 (2002)

F. Scripture and Ethics

See first the general introduction to the Bible in this series, Benedict Hegarty, *The Bible: Literature and Sacred Text*, Dublin, Veritas, 2003. On biblical interpretation see essays in John Barton, *The Cambridge Companion to Biblical Interpretation*, Cambridge, 1998. On biblical ethics see especially the excellent essay by Tom Deidun, 'The Bible and Christian Ethics', in B. Hoose (ed.), *Christian Ethics: an Introduction*, London, 1998, 3ff., which also contains ample reference. For modern interpretations by moral theologians of the concept of Christian discipleship see Timothy O'Connell, *Making Disciples,* New York, 1998, and William C. Spohn, *Go and Do Likewise: Jesus and Ethics*, New York, 2000. A challenging short account of the moral teaching of Jesus is Nicholas Peter Harvey, *The Morals of Jesus*, London, 1991.

G. Morality and Spirituality

Cunningham, Lawrence, and Egan, Keith, *Christian Spirituality, Themes from the Tradition*, New York/Mahwah, 1996

Downey, Michael, *Understanding Christian Spirituality*, New York/Mahwah, 1997

MacNamara, Vincent, *New Life for Old: On Desire and Becoming Human*, Dublin, 2004

McGrath, Alister, *Christian Spirituality: On Introduction*, Oxford, 1999

Sheldrake, Philip, *Spirituality and History*, London, 1991

Sheldrake, Philip, *Spirituality and Theology*, London, 1998

H. Catholic Church Teaching

Catechism of the Catholic Church, Dublin, 1994

Vatican Council Two: Constitutions, Decrees, Declarations, ed. A. Flannery, Dublin, 1996

Veritatis Splendor, Dublin, 1993

Other titles in the

INTO THE CLASSROOM SERIES

RELIGION – THE IRISH EXPERIENCE

J. R. Walsh

J.R. Walsh surveys the religious experience of the Irish people through the ages. Including a discussion of the influence of the monastic movement on the Church in Ireland and the connections between land and religion, the author also explores the impact of Enlightenment thinking in Europe and in Ireland, and the development of a diversity of belief in modern Ireland. *Religion: The Irish Experience* is a stimulating introduction to a fascinating topic.

1 85390 684 0 • €12.95

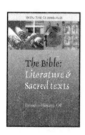

THE BIBLE – LITERATURE AND SACRED TEXTS

Benedict Hegarty OP

The Bible is both the foundation text of the Christian faith and one of the key documents of human civilisation. However, it emerged from a place, time and culture that can seem remote to the twenty-first century reader. This book is designed to help just such a reader by situating it in context.

Including close analysis of important texts from the Old and New Testaments, *The Bible: Literature & Sacred Texts* brings the world of the Bible to life for the modern reader.

1 85390 679 4 • €12.95

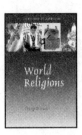

WORLD RELIGIONS
Philip Barnes

As Ireland becomes increasingly multicultural, many people wish to learn more about the religions and cultures that are becoming part of our society. In this clearly-written, informative book Philip Barnes outlines the tenets and beliefs of all the major world religions, devoting chapters to the nature of religion, Judaism, Christianity, Islam, Hinduism, Buddhism and New Religious Movements, and explaining them in the context of their history and culture. The role of religion in causing and sustaining religious conflict is also examined, particularly in relation to the conflicts in Northern Ireland and the Middle East. A valuable and enlightening resource for the educator and general reader alike.

1 85390 701 4 • €14.95

THE SEARCH FOR MEANING AND VALUES
Eoin G. Cassidy

The Search for Meaning and Values is divided into four parts: the first focuses on the context within which the search for meaning and values takes place, the second on the response to the quest for meaning and values, the third on belief in God as a locus for this quest, and the fourth on the manner in which religion both responds to and shapes these great questions of life.

1 85390 689 1 • €14.95